TWICE A CHAMPION
The Toney Lineberry Story

by
Tommy Lineberry

Copyright 1988 by Fred Thomas Lineberry
and Anthony Wayne Lineberry

All rights reserved. No part of this book may be reproduced in any form without written permission from the authors, except by a reviewer and/or the press who may quote brief passages in a review to be printed in a newspaper or magazine.

Cover design by Scott Fields and Robin Baxter, Carter Printing Co.

Cover Photo: Two days before Toney's accident.

Inset cover photo by Fred Kenderson

Edited by Frederick Talbott, Old Dominion University

Library of Congress Catalog Card Number: 88-91090

First Printing March 1988
Second Printing May 1988
by Carter Printing Co.
United States of America

DEDICATION

I don't know how some authors are able to choose just one person to dedicate their books to. I couldn't, so I have several.

To my sisters, their husbands and all my little nieces and nephews. You mean more to me than words can describe. You are all a part of this book.

To my friends (Mike, Jeff, and Brauma) for saying I couldn't do it. Thanks for giving me that extra little incentive.

To Fred Talbott, my professor, my editor, and my friend. Thanks for your infinite wisdom.

To my mama and daddy. You are everything I am and will ever be. I hope this book preserves in everyones' heart just how special you two are.

To Donna, for being my brother's wife. Sometimes I think God put you on this earth just to bring happiness into our lives.

Finally, with all my heart, to Toney. I've always wanted to be just like you. Now, after all you've overcome, after all the people you've touched, I'd just like to be half the man that you are. You're still my hero.

Tommy

DEDICATION

Over the past several months while Tommy and I have been working on this book many memories have been stirred, some bad, but many good. During that time I've had the opportunity to take a close look at the events that have shaped my life.

Every chapter has reminded me of someone or some group that has helped me deal with my disability. The biggest fear I had the whole time was who will be left out? Who's feelings will be hurt? There have been so many people who have helped me and become my friends, that it became clear in the very beginning that it would be impossible to name every person or recall every event. So, I wanted to take this opportunity to apologize to those whose names might have been left out. You know who you are and I trust you also realize that I am grateful for all of the kindness, understanding and support that I've been showered with. You are now and will always be in my thoughts and close to my heart. I thank you.

I would also like to give credit to a few very special people in my life.

To my in-laws, the Brocks: I thank you for the way you have welcomed me into your family with open arms. You have always seen me for my ability and not my disability. For this, I am grateful.

To my three older sisters, Terry, Cathy, and Donna: You've always paved the way for me and made my life easier. You share your families with me and that brings me joy and happiness. For these things and more, I love you.

To my brother, Tommy: Several months ago when I said, "I would like to put all of this in a book" you said, "I can write it!" I never doubted it. We have spent countless hours talking and planning, you've spent many more writing. You have shown energy and enthusiasm. Without you, there is no way this book would've been written. I don't think I could've shared these feelings and emotions with anyone else. You are not only my brother, but also my friend. I love you.

To my mother, Eva: You gave me life and taught me right from wrong. After my crash there were many times when I cried, but somehow you turned the tears into laughter. During my darkest times, when I was down, you lifted me up. You helped me learn how to deal with and accept my disability. You are the world's greatest mom. I love you.

To my father, Don: When I was a boy, I always enjoyed spending time with you and going places together. That hasn't changed. Even today, I cherish the time we spend with each other. Any time I have a problem, you help me solve it. You have always been there for me. Few know what you've been through and what we have overcome together. However, I know. And I am proud to claim you as my father. You are the world's greatest dad. I love you.

To my wife, Donna: It doesn't seem like words are enough to express the way I feel about you. Not only are you my wife, you're also my partner and best friend. You are the sunshine in my life. Without you, it would all be meaningless. You make my life worth living. The things I do, I do for you. You are the best thing that has ever happened to me. I love you.

While this book was being written, our sister Cathy gave birth to a baby boy, Tatum. When he was ten months old, we learned that he had a cancerous tumor. It was a grim reminder to me of how quickly things can change and how the ones we love become threatened. While I was sitting with him at the hospital, I realized, once again, how precious life really is. He doesn't understand his pain, and I guess we don't either. Through his pain and agony he has remained strong. After two operations and many other complications that came along with cancer, he continues to smile, laugh, and grow, even while receiving chemotherapy. In my eyes, he is also a champion! And for that reason, I dedicate this book to him.

Toney

CONTENTS

CHAPTER 1
TONEY WITH AN EY — 1

CHAPTER 2
THE ACCIDENT — 9

CHAPTER 3
HE'LL NEVER WALK AGAIN — 21

CHAPTER 4
THE STRUGGLE CONTINUES — 39

CHAPTER 5
WHY ME? — 53

CHAPTER 6
ANOTHER HOSPITAL — 69

CHAPTER 7
THE DREAM — 85

CHAPTER 8
SO, WHAT ARE YOU GONNA DO NOW? — 125

CHAPTER 9
BUCKLE UP FOR TONEY — 145

CHAPTER 10
A FULL LIFE — 165

CHAPTER 11
STILL A CHAMPION — 185

CHAPTER 1
TONEY WITH AN EY

*S*now covered the ground as I followed mama through the parking lot at St. Luke's Hospital. It seemed to swallow my feet as I trudged down the long sidewalk. Sleet peppered my nose. I had trouble keeping my eyes open as the wind burned my face.

I was twelve. Sleigh riding was on my mind. My brother should have been on my mind. He was inside, weak, in critical condition.

My family was also inside. They sat in the waiting room, consoling each other and thinking. They thought about the strong Toney, the Toney they were missing so much.

* * * * *

Toney was a name everyone knew in Laurel Park. If you lived there in the seventies, he probably delivered your newspaper on his unicycle, mowed your lawn for five bucks, or kissed your daughter behind the shopping center.

Toney lived a very happy middle-class childhood. He had parents who cared. He had three older sisters to fight with and a little brother to pick on. I used to wonder if I would always be five years younger than him.

Mama spelled Toney with an EY because that's how she thought it was spelled. When she found out that the E was not necessary, she kept it. She kept it, she said, because her son was different. His name deserved individuality.

He stood out from the crowd. He was loud and hyper. He was a competitor. He seemed to take pride in everything he did.

He hated to lose. From "Old Maid" to little league football, he seemed to always be a winner.

When he reached junior high school Toney became very well known as an athlete. Sports were the most important thing in his life. He spent countless hours trying to build his body up. He was obsessed with being in shape. He felt that his body was his main asset.

He ran track and gave it all he had. He wasn't the fastest by any means, but his heart and determination won him several ribbons.

He played football and seemed to always be the smallest player —and hardest hitter—on the field. He viciously patrolled his defensive back position.

Toney found his real love on the wrestling mat. From the day of his first tryout, he knew this was the sport for him. He decided he would become the best.

I remember sitting on the edge of my bed at nights. I would count sit-ups and push-ups for Toney as I waited for the lights to be cut off. He was so strong to me. He would make a muscle and I would swing from it as he walked through the house.

Toney was more determined to become a great wrestler than anything else. He rolled around a wrestling mat or in our back yard every day trying to perfect moves he had learned. We all knew that someday he would be a champion.

Daddy is a bus driver. When not traveling the interstates of Virginia, his favorite hobby was watching Toney wrestle. Veins would pop out on his forehead as he balled up his fist and screamed at Toney.

"Push it!"

Very seldom did daddy drive home a loser.

Toney went undefeated and won the 112 pound county championship in the eighth grade. He was growing and his muscular body was beginning to look more and more like steel. He headed for high school with a can't-miss tag on him.

Hermitage High School was another world compared to Brookland Junior High. It had a huge stadium with tall, bright lights. It had several parking lots filled with the cars of kids who actually drove to school. It had a weight room that was a body builder's paradise. And an athletic program unsurpassed in the area.

Hermitage also has a very highly acclaimed academic program. Toney didn't know or care about this, however. He was more concerned with meeting the wrestling coach and visiting the weight room than with making the honor roll.

Toney had a girlfriend. They thought they were in love, that they had found the perfect mate. They thought they would spend the rest of their lives together. Only time would tell.

Toney used his time at school to spend with his girl and his other friends. He studied only enough to pass his classes, only because "You can't wrestle if you fail."

Toney was actually very intelligent. He had the ability to make good grades. He just never realized that he wouldn't be able to wrestle forever.

On the night of his wrestling matches he would just growl and think about his opponent. There was no tomorrow, nothing else mattered. This attitude made him a great wrestler, but it harmed him in the classroom.

Toney did work hard in one class. He studied hard in driver's education trying to get high grades. The students with the highest grades were the first to get their driver's licenses. Toney dreamed of the day he could cruise around Richmond with his girlfriend by his side.

Toney worked hard trying to get the high grades in driver's ed., but he still didn't take the class seriously. He would sit in the class, a friend or two on each side, and watch gory safety films. They would show deadly crashes. Bloody passengers would be thrown through windshields. Limbs would be pinned under cars.

"That's a joke," he'd think. "It'll never happen to me."

When the bell rang, Toney and his friends would grab their lunch bags and run for the door, slugging each other on the arm on the way out.

Toney got an "A" in drivers ed. and soon got his drivers license. He borrowed dad's car often and spent hours just driving around. He would pick up his friends and cruise Broad Street. He and his girl would take in a drive-in movie.

The excitement of having his license wore off and Toney entered the second stage that most teenage drivers hit: He wanted his own car.

Toney didn't want just any car. He had in his mind the car of his dreams. He would sit under the oak tree in our front yard, chewing on a weed, and envision it. It was a red sports car with black racing stripes and mag wheels. He wanted that car more than anything.

Toney got a job at the Exxon station up the street. Daddy agreed to help him buy a car. He finally got the car of his dreams, a 1969 Ford Mustang.

Toney worked hard and saved for those mag wheels and that red paint job. I'll never forget the day he drove the car home from the body shop. He drove slowly down Stockbridge Drive. His arm rested on the rolled-down window and he had sunglasses on. The car seemed filled with teeth as he grinned his way into our driveway.

The car was beautiful. It shined like a clear lake on a sunny afternoon. You could see yourself in it, plain as day. I stood beside it and made faces at myself.

Toney washed the car every day, whether it needed it or not. He made people take their shoes off when riding in it. It was his pride and joy, the one thing he cared about most.

Toney was absolutely awesome on the wrestling mat. He was lightning quick. Weighing only 112 pounds, he could bench press 250 pounds. We used to kid that he had muscles on his muscles.

Toney moved up to the 119 pound weight class in his junior year. He learned to be a leader as he was chosen co-captain of his team.

He was like an animal on the mat, winning match after match. He was undefeated and there was talk of a state championship at season's end.

Toney was gifted with physical talent, and he became polished with the help of his high school coach, Tim Donahue. Coach Donahue wasn't the type of coach who just shouted instructions from the side with a whistle around his neck. He liked to get in there and wrestle. He and Toney spent many sweaty afternoons trying to mold Toney into a champion.

As Toney remained undefeated, a kid from a rival high school was doing equally well. Hermitage was scheduled to wrestle this high school in the final match of the season. The match was to include a clash between the two best 119 pounders in the district. It would determine the number one seed in the upcoming district tournament.

Toney wanted to win this match, and to win big. He was determined to prove that he was the best.

He trained night and day for the match. He ate, slept, and thought wrestling. He trained as if nothing else mattered. He trained as if this match would be to the death.

I stared at Toney as he paced back and forth past our T.V. on the afternoon before the big match. His legs looked like tree trunks as they blocked my view of "The Flintstones." I didn't dare tell him to get out of the way.

His hair was parted in the middle. He had a ferocious gleam in his eyes and he didn't smile. He wore a tank-top shirt that seemed surrounded by muscles. Every once in a while his forehead would wrinkle and he'd pound his hand with his fist. I flinched with each "pop," and felt relieved that I would not be his victim that night.

Toney stood beside the wrestling mat, his arms swinging limp, as if to relax himself. He adjusted his head gear as his name was announced.

"At 119 for Hermitage, co-captain, Toe-neee Lineberry!"

Toney didn't hear the P.A. announcer. He just stared into his opponents eyes and growled.

When the whistle blew, Toney swept in and immediately took the kid to the mat. You could hear him "ouch" as Toney twisted his limbs in different directions. He scored point after point. He would take him down and let him up, flip him here and flip him there.

It was a thrashing decision. Toney was now the only undefeated 119 pounder in his district.

The crowd stood and roared and daddy stood proud with his arms crossed. His face was tomato red. He looked as though he had wrestled.

Toney jumped into his teammates' arms and thrust his fists into the air. He was the best, no doubt about it.

With the satisfaction of his victory still glowing in his eyes, Toney prepared to celebrate a day that he had been waiting for his entire life. It was the day he considered himself to be grown up. It was the day when he could make his own decisions, be responsible for his own actions. He stared in the mirror at the "H" on his sweatshirt. Today he was a man.

We sang "Happy Birthday" as Toney blew out the eighteen candles on his cake. He seemed almost arrogant as he extinguished the candles with a tiny puff.

Toney polished his car, then lifted weights on the afternoon of his birthday. He stood there, curling one hundred pounds, and thought. He thought about how great it was to be eighteen. He thought about how great his future would be.

He slammed down his weights and stared up into the sky.

"There's no stopping me now!"

* * * * *

Eight days later I made that awful visit to St. Luke's Hospital.

I didn't know what to expect as my older sister pointed me towards Toney in the intensive care unit. I slowly walked up to his stretcher, looking for my big, strong, eighteen-year-old brother. For some reason, I looked for muscles and a wrestling uniform. They weren't there. Instead, on that hideous table, was a stranger. His head was shaven. Cuts and gashes covered him. He stared straight up and had trouble breathing.

I was cold and my teeth began to chatter. I folded my arms around myself and stared at my brother.

Until six hours ago he was the strongest person I knew. Now he just lay there, helpless, a mannequin named Toney.

There was nothing I could do. I fell to my knees and began to cry. My sister gently scooped me up and carried me out of the room as I cried on her shoulder. I wondered what was wrong with my brother. I didn't realize he was dying.

CHAPTER 2
THE ACCIDENT

I didn't sleep much that night. I squirmed in my bed as a million thoughts rushed through my mind. I thought about how hectic this day had been. I thought about all the sadness I had witnessed.

Mostly I thought about one memorable, snowy day. I loved that snow. I couldn't stop thinking about that day. I relived it over and over in my mind . . . .

The sky was a puff of white powder. Ice dripped from the trees and tapped at our window. A myriad of beautiful snowflakes floated down from the sky. I felt my smile getting wider as each one hit the ground.

Toney and I shared a small bedroom. Football posters lined the walls. A stand with dozens of Toney's trophies dominated a corner. We had twin beds. A table with a clock radio on it sat between them. Wrestling gear was piled at the end of Toney's bed and stuffed animals at the end of mine.

A pile of dirty clothes was forming by the window. It peeked over the sash and its shadow looked like a mountain as the snow fell behind it.

Toney and I sat on the edge of our beds, his big feet sunk in the carpet, my pajamaed legs dangling, and listened intently to the D.J. on the clock radio waiting to see if our schools would be closed. He talked for what seemed like hours about snow accumulations, weather forecasts, and how bad the road conditions were. Finally the news came: Henrico County Schools would be closed that day. Toney and I were thrilled! I don't think we hated school that much, we just loved the idea of being home. It would give me a chance to lie around and watch all my favorite game shows. Toney would have a break from his busy schedule. We jumped around in our room and ran into the hall.

Our parents didn't seem to be as thrilled. They were getting ready for work. They didn't like the thought of driving in the storm. I suppose mama was wondering what shape her house would be in when she got home.

This was a scene that had been repeated down through the years, but there was always one of my sisters around the house to keep things straight. This time Terry and Cathy were away. Terry was teaching in Southwest Virginia and Cathy was away at college. Donna had been married for two years and had just had a brand new baby. On this day it was just twelve-year-old me and my big superstar brother free to wreck the house. We were as happy as two frogs in a swamp.

Mama and daddy left for work and our spectacular "home from school day" began. I cut on the "Price is Right" and kicked back. I planned to watch the tube until the soap operas came on then get in some sleigh riding. Toney was already on the phone with his girlfriend and had plans to go shopping with Coach Donahue that day.

I remember the boredom of the day setting in early. The game shows got old and Toney and I slowly began picking at each other. I'd flick his ear. He'd scrub my head with his fist. I'd say his girlfriend was ugly. He'd twist my arm behind my back. I'd crawl under the chair and listen in on his phone conversations. He'd slam me against the wall. It was a normal snowed-in morning around the house.

Coach Donahue picked Toney up in the afternoon and they went to Disco Sports to look at the latest in wrestling gear. They talked about the district tournament coming up and Toney couldn't help but think to himself that he couldn't lose. After all, he just destroyed his closest competitor. They shopped around some more and Toney found a stereo tape box and some headphones he wanted. He decided to wait and buy them for himself for winning the district.

The coach dropped Toney off at the house and reminded him

practice would start early the next morning. I had gotten some sleigh riding in while Toney was gone, but I was back when he returned. I remember looking at him as he came through the door with his heavy, brown, suede jacket and brand-new Christmas cowboy boots on. He looked like a mountain, and I wondered if I should call his girlfriend a goat or not. I decided not to, but fifteen minutes later I called her pine-needle head and he slammed me on top of mom's rubber tree. We didn't speak the rest of the day.

The afternoon dragged on. Match Game '78 at 3:30, Hawaii Five-O at four. Mama got home at five. She came through the door taking off her ice-covered coat, shaking the sleet out of her "mama's" hairdo and telling us about how the icy rain had started up again. She said she saw several people sliding into each other in the parking lot and that she had seen lots of wrecks on the way home. For Toney it was in one ear and out the other. Mama made it home, it couldn't be but so bad.

Daddy came in with the same stories. Coming from a professional driver you would think it would sink in, but it didn't.

I'll never forget dinner that night. We had what we always had, a roast, mashed potatoes, and green beans. Mama was a fabulous cook. She would turn those ordinary, middle-class meals into a Henry the VIII feast. We sat there munching away. As always, daddy was at the head of the table, Toney was at the other end, mama was on the side next to the phone, and I was on the other side.

When the meal was about done the phone rang. Mom got up, answered it, and informed Toney that it was for him. Toney got the phone, bent the cord around the door into the living room, and talked for a while. I figured it was just his girlfriend yacking away, but when he returned to the table he told mama and daddy it was a buddy of his and that he was going out that night.

Immediately mama and daddy chimed in and said "No way! There's no way you're going out in this mess!"

Toney looked at them funny. Daddy said "Hell boy, you'll tear your car up."

"Listen to your daddy, Toney. You're not going out." Mama added.

Toney bolted. "Yes I am."

They said. "No you're not."

He countered. "Yes I am!"

Toney jumped up, slammed his chair against the table and stormed off to his room.

My parents were never strict with us, but they were always concerned about our personal welfare. There was no doubt in their minds that Toney was not going to take the car that night.

Dad was usually a silent force. Mom did the actual "saying no" and dad would step in when necessary. They were a good team.

When mom went back to our room to talk with Toney he was combing his hair. He stood there with that same look he had on his 18th birthday, a look that said "nobody is going to tell me what to do!" He combed his hair with power and didn't even look at mom. As always, she didn't like seeing him upset.

"O.K. Toney, your dad and I have decided we're going to let you go out," she said.

Toney just snickered. He knew they would see it his way.

"We're going to let you go out, but you're not taking the car."

It started again. "Yes I am."

"No you're not."

"Yes I am."

Then dad stepped in the room. He gave Toney one of his famous snarls, and Toney said, "Okay, I won't take it!"

Mom and dad were sitting on the couch when Toney's cowboy boots clunked down the hall. His face was wrinkled with anger as he grabbed his coat off the piano. Mom and dad just watched as he left, slamming the door behind him, not saying a word. I'm sure mom and dad felt disturbed by his anger, but relieved that he was on foot.

The plan was to meet his friend at the top of the street and take it from there. This was a common scene. Toney would often pick up his friend on weekend nights when he wasn't out with his girlfriend. But tonight was a common scene, with a twist: Toney had no wheels.

His friend bellowed. "Hey man, why are you walking?"

"You know how mama and daddy are. Sometimes the roads get a little wet and they think I don't know how to drive!"

"Isn't it your car?! Didn't you just turn 18?!"

Toney was not easily influenced and rarely pressured by his peers. He didn't smoke cigarettes or take drugs, and only drank when he wanted to. His athletics and taking care of his body were too important. But his friend struck a nerve that night, he put Toney on the defensive.

No one was going to tell him he couldn't take his car.

The two decided they would kill some time until mom and dad went to bed, then they would go back to the house and get the car. It had stopped snowing but the roads were still wet and slick in places.

As they approached the house Toney motioned for his friend to wait by the car. He crawled towards the window, through the bushes, and over the flower bed. A quick peek through the living room window was all it took, the coast was clear. Mama and daddy had gone to bed.

While his friend pushed, Toney steered the car out of the driveway and to the end of the street. He must have known that what he was doing was wrong, but he did it anyway. His friend hopped in and they were on their way. The car fishtailed a little from the ice, but Toney was in control, the steering wheel was right there in his hand and the brake and gas were right there at his feet.

They decided that the thing to do was ride up to the local hangout and see what was going on. In those days the hangout was McDonalds. You could always ride through the parking lot on a Friday or Saturday night and see dozens of kids sitting on the hoods of their cars or huddled in a booth inside. This is a scene that has been common down through the years. From the drive-in restaurants of the fifties to the dragstrip hangouts of today. The hair styles and cars have changed, but the kids are the same.

With the heater in the Mustang going full blast, Toney and his friend sat silently in a parking space. None of their friends were around. As an eight-track tape of the Doobie Brothers played,

Toney sat and thought how he would like the night to turn out. He decided that he wouldn't drink any beer that night. Wrestling practice was first thing in the morning. He thought he'd like to find some of his friends and socialize the night away, get the car back before mama and daddy woke up, and get a good nights sleep.

Just then a brand new 1978 Firebird pulled into the parking lot. Toney and his friend recognized it as one of their buddy's and his friend scarfed down his cheeseburger in excitement. They jumped out of the warm Mustang into the frosty air and waved them down.

The Firebird pulled into the space next to the Mustang. Even in chilling weather that car of Toney's looked hot. As the door of the Firebird flung open guys piled out everywhere. Beer cans fell here, liquor bottles there. It seemed like there were about ten guys in the car. It was obvious they were having a great time. Not being able to stand it anymore, Toney yelled out, "Hey man, what's going on?!"

"It's a great party, Lineberry. You're missing it!"

"Well, where is it?"

"Man it's an awesome party, plenty of booze, women you're missing it!"

"Well, where is it?"

"They just decided to have it about two hours ago, everybody's there, you're missing it!"

Toney's friend jumped in the conversation in frustration.

"Where the hell's the party?!"

The partying pal got the point. "You go up here to the highway and take a right, go about two miles 'til you pass the junior high, go a little further past the community college and it'll be your first set of apartments on the right. You'll see Mike's van and Danny's Dodge, you can't miss it. Hurry, you're missing it!"

This was great. They had found a party, the joy of all high school kids. They jumped in the 'Stang and were on their way. There was a patch of ice on the edge of the parking lot and the car fishtailed going out. Toney was in control though, the steering wheel was right there in his hand and the brake and gas were right there at his feet.

The ride to the party seemed like hours to the boys. Toney put in the Eagle's *Hotel California* tape as the car sped down the highway, occasionally plowing through a pile of slush. His friend was swigging beers and shimmying to the music as he talked about what fine young ladies might be at this party. Toney was excited, but couldn't forget about mama and daddy. He wished they were jamming in someone else's car. He thought about wrestling practice that next morning and how Coach Donahue probably wouldn't like it if he knew he was out.

An occasional flurry of snow would drop on the hood of the car as it soared down the highway. The directions to the party were perfect. The junior high was up ahead on the left. Toney could see the light at Brookland and his eighth grade county championship match popped into his head. Memories of his girlfriend and him running to class seemed to flash across the sky. He shook his head and thought in fond remembrance of "old" Brookland.

The car moved on past the school and over a hill. Toney was searching for the community college when he saw up ahead what looked like a river flowing across the road. Maybe not a river, but whatever it was it was a large body of water. There was lots of light glaring down out of the sky onto it. It seemed to glow with the reflection from a nearby building. The water had a strong look about it. It looked almost alive.

The water didn't phase Toney. He had conquered much bigger opponents in his lifetime. He instinctively gave the car a little gas and sped towards it.

Suddenly, Toney's conceit turned to horror. He screamed. His friend grabbed the dashboard and ducked his head.

It was a solid sheet of ice.

When the front wheels of the car hit the ice it spun out of control. The car spun like a top and Toney's forehead smashed the side window and then the dash. His arms flopped uncontrollably, like spaghetti, and his legs flipped over his shoulder. He struggled and reached, but there was nothing to grab. He was completely out of control. The brake and gas pedals were no longer at his feet. The steering wheel was no longer in his hand. A flying seat belt slapped him across the face. The force of the spin sucked all the air from his lungs.

The monstrous patch of ice seemed to heave the Mustang through the air. The car tumbled violently, over and over. Blood spewed from Toney's forehead. He bounced around as each part of his body took a beating. For the first time in his life, there was nothing his muscular body could do for him.

The force threw his friend through the windshield, then jerked him back through the jagged glass as if the car was toying with him. A bone jutted through his shoulder and his eyes rolled to the back of his head as he plunged into shock.

Glass was blasting from all the windows. It ripped their faces as their bodies collided.

The Mustang was reduced to a giant, red snow flurry on this night. The boys inside were two uncontrolled bodies, tumbling around like loose change in a clothes dryer.

The car finally rammed a lone pine tree and slid upside down into a ravine.

The mangled piece of steel lay smoking, almost heaving in the bowels of that cold and uninviting hole. Toney was lying there, crushed, with the steering column wrapped around his body. He thought it was a dream, a nightmare. He just knew he would wake up any minute and see the clock radio beside his bed.

It was not a dream. The Mustang was swaying on its top. Toney gasped for air as a small stream flowed over his neck. There was an awful sewer smell. Pain shot through him as if he were being stabbed. His eyes watered as he tried to fight it.

A million thoughts rushed through Toney's mind. He thought about his paper route. He thought about his month-old nephew. He thought about those gory tenth-grade driver's education films, how they were always a joke and how "it'll never happen to me." Now they weren't a joke. He was playing the lead role in one of those films.

He was dying.

Interior parts of the car seemed to squeeze Toney like a vice. He tried desperately to move his body, but he couldn't. A bloody leg was twisted around his neck like a noose. An arm was swirled around his chest. Toney thought they were his friends limbs, that he had been dismembered during the crash. All he could see of his friend was his bloody neck and shoulder hunched over the seat. He knew he was dead.

Toney tried to let out a scream but couldn't get enough air in his lungs. He was cold and trembled all over. He wondered if he was dead too, if this was the way death felt.

Suddenly, he heard a car and people yelling. He tried again to scream. Air was coming harder and harder and only a squeak came out.

It was incredibly dark down in that hole. It seemed like days for Toney while he tried desperately to remove the bloody limbs that were wrapped around him.

Suddenly, the darkness burst into a rush of blinding light. People surrounded the mass of mangled metal that was once a red Mustang. Rescue workers seemed to attack the car.

"Put that cigarette out!"

"Don't move him!"

Toney was frightened beyond control. He had a shock-like pain in his neck. He wondered if he would ever get his friend's limbs off of him. He wondered if he would ever get out of this hole.

A short, baldheaded man crawled through the hole in the wreckage to cover him with a sheet to protect him from flying glass. The little guy was the only one small enough to fit in the hole. He consoled Toney and told him not to worry, help had arrived.

The workers used a "jaws of life" to pop Toney's door open. As they carefully began to free him from the wreckage, Toney saw the bloody limbs flop down beside him. They weren't his friend's limbs at all. They were his, but he couldn't feel them.

Toney was still in a daze. This couldn't be happening.

He couldn't be carried out of the ravine by a mere stretcher for the fear of risking more damage. He was cradled onto a hook-and-ladder from a fire engine and hoisted out of the ravine. High in the air, as he was moving upward, he wondered if he was floating to heaven. He saw what looked like an arena of people below.

Soon he was in an ambulance speeding toward St. Luke's Hospital. He couldn't feel anything and his neck throbbed with pain. The siren hurt his ear and he wished he were unconscious.

The stretcher carrying one of the state's best wrestlers was unloaded at the hospital. A body of steel couldn't move. An eighteen-year-old boy, who two hours earlier had life clutched in his palm, was gasping for air. The emergency room door burst open.

"This one's next. He's in bad shape!"

CHAPTER 3
HE'll NEVER WALK AGAIN

*M*ama and daddy had the bedroom at the end of the hall in our house. I suppose because it was within easy striking distance of either my and Toney's room or the girl's room. I can remember pulling them out of bed by their robes on many a Christmas morning.

I'm sure mama was wiping sleep from her eyes as she walked down the hall to answer the doorbell late that Friday night. She opened the heavy wood door and saw, through the "L" on the screen door, a man in blue wearing a badge that was dripping with icy rain. Still trying to wake up, she was not prepared for what the officer had to say.

"Mrs. Lineberry?"

"Yes."

"I'm sorry to be the one to have to tell you this. Your son, Anthony Wayne, has been in an automobile accident."

"Is he okay?"

"They don't know if he's going to make it."

Terror flashed in mama's eyes as she snapped back. "That's impossible! He didn't even drive tonight!"

She ran over to the window and pulled the curtain back. The empty driveway made her heart drop to her stomach. She let out a murmur of a cry and fell into a chair.

The officer stepped into the house as daddy came in the room, tying his robe. He expected the worst after he saw mama and that badge.

The officer gave daddy the hospital information as mama wept in the chair. The man left and daddy consoled mama. Their lives would be changed forever.

I never awoke as they wept in the front room. Mama soon

opened my bedroom door to tell me that they were going to the hospital and I'm not sure that I even awoke then. My drowsiness wouldn't allow me to notice her tears. I snuggled my head back in the pillow, whispering "Okay, see ya later."

St. Luke's Hospital seemed a cold and dreary place to mom and dad. It was quiet. They could hear the echo of their footsteps as they hurried down the long hallway towards the intensive care unit.

Toney was conscious, but couldn't move at all. He could only see straight up. He had no idea what was wrong with him and he assumed he'd be better in a couple of days.

Mama is a strong woman. She refused to let Toney see her cry, wiping a tear as she walked through the door. She had only positive things to say. She must have said "You're gonna be all right" a million times. As she leaned over the stretcher to get within his view, Toney gave her a painful smile. He asked her to call Coach Donahue and tell him that he would probably miss practice that morning.

Suddenly, a terrifying thought entered Toney's mind. He burst into hysterics and screamed.

"Oh God, mama! Did I kill him?"

Toney remembered his bloody friend drooped over a seat, unconcious. He remembered thinking his pal was dead.

"No honey. He's gonna be fine," mama said. "He's just cut up and he has a broken collar bone. He's gonna be fine. Don't worry honey, just get some rest."

Our father has always been a strong man. His emotions rarely changed to a great degree, except when we messed up the leaves he had raked and he would put a work boot into our rumps. I was sure he was emotional, but I don't think he wanted anyone to see it.

Toney saw him cry for the first time that morning. It made Toney cry and they wept together. Toney's athletic ability perhaps meant more to daddy than to anyone. There would be no wrestling on this day.

I woke up that morning with a terrible feeling. I remembered mama saying she was going to the hospital and I was terrified that someone was hurt bad, or even dead. I knew something was very wrong when relatives started showing up. My cousin Milton and his wife were first. They took me to Hardee's for breakfast. It must be very difficult to tell a twelve-year-old boy that his brother is in critical condition. They tried very hard but I'm not sure it sunk in. I ate my biscuit and assumed Toney would be home later on in the day.

I began to wonder even more when my eighty-year-old grandmother arrived. She lived three hundred miles away and rarely left her farm. We visited her often, but she hadn't visited us in years.

My sisters were rounded up immediately. They were very hard to get in touch with, but through several channels the message finally got to them. They were all shocked, but in different ways.

Cathy's only thoughts of Toney were of her big, strong, wrestling brother. He could take care of himself, he would be all right.

Terry was scared to death. A close friend of hers had been in an accident just six years before. His back was broken and he would spend the rest of his life in a wheelchair. Terry was bouncing off the walls as her boyfriend, C.B., drove her home. She feared Toney would end up like her friend.

My sister Donna was in close range and was the first that mama called. Donna was always like a mother to Toney and me. The news hit her hard. She had a one-month-old baby boy at the time but somehow managed to stay by mama's side throughout the early hours.

Toney's girlfriend stayed with him a lot in the beginning. She and her family spent many hours either by his side, or in the waiting room with my family. They were a great help as we all speculated about Toney's fate.

Pain was ringing through Toney's body like electricity. His neck had a constant, shocking pain. His head throbbed as if it was about to explode. For the first time in his life there was no feeling of strength, no feeling of control. Every feeling was of pain.

Toney's body was a bundle of red, black, and blue. His face was a mass of lacerations and his neck and shoulders were as black and blue as a coal miner in the Union Army. His body was covered with open gashes and bits of glass. Both his eyes were black and blood still dripped from the corner of his mouth. He was not a pretty sight in those early hours.

He had to be immobilized immediately. A neck injury is a delicate thing and the hard stretcher was already taking its toll. The doctors ordered that Toney be put on a striker frame, a bed of metal suspended in air. The patient's body is completely exposed to avoid bedsores. The bed is periodically rotated from front to back to keep circulation moving.

The patient's legs are strapped to the bed at one end, and his head is bolted to the other end to keep the neck in traction, completely immobile. Thumb-sized bolts are screwed into the skull and into a metal "halo" which is attached to the bed.

Being put on the frame was a horrifying experience for Toney. He was heavily sedated but somewhat aware as a nurse ran an electric razor over his head. Tears spewed from his eyes. He heard a crackling noise as the bolts were being screwed into his skull.

Weight was to be attached to his head in order to keep his neck in a safe position. Thirty pounds was attached, but the pressure on the neck seemed like a ton to Toney. He had lifted weights before and thirty pounds seemed like an incredibly small amount then. Now it was enough to make his eyes water and his neck pulsate with pain.

Despite all the pain and suffering that Toney was going through, the hardest thing, the truly hardest thing, was that he couldn't feel or move his body. He couldn't scratch himself. He couldn't get a glass of water. He couldn't hug his girlfriend. He couldn't move. And no one would tell him why. He couldn't get a straight answer. He feared the worst.

The sad fact is not many people knew exactly what was wrong. The doctors repeatedly filled mama and daddy with lots of medical jargon about critical condition and life threatening situations. They finally waited until they were sure before pulling mama and daddy aside. "Toney has broken his neck between the fifth and sixth vertebrae. He will never walk again."

Mama began to weep, but she never lost hope. She sat by Toney's side, a daughter or two always with her. She was determined that he would not lose hope either.

A glimmer of strength remained in Toney. He used it all to look as good as he possibly could for his visitors. He couldn't let them see Toney Lineberry, champion wrestler, down. He would get tired, but never sleep if there was someone to see.

He would only let mama see him cry. She would sit by his striker frame, day after day, and smother him with love. She kept a box of tissues in her lap and wiped his tears. She was the only one he could let know he was down.

Every visit was important in those early days. Several were special.

On that somber morning of the crash, our brother-in-law, Mike Koehler, went in to see Toney. Mike was also a great athlete at Hermitage and Toney admired him immensely. They always shared an athletic bond. Their relationship was built on mutual respect. Mike had married Donna two years earlier and he became a solid, permanent part of our family.

Mike is strong and witty. He's always the rock in times of despair, always ready with a joke to lighten the mood. On this day, however, he broke down.

He couldn't stand to see Toney like that. This time it was Toney's turn to lighten the mood. He asked Mike if little Mike was okay. Mike couldn't even answer. He covered his eyes and left the room. It hit him that Toney wouldn't be able to enjoy the usual "uncle to nephew" times.

In the weeks to come Mike would not break down again. He would often pose as a fat man and sneak little Mike in under his shirt to see Toney.

Visits from wrestling teammates were hard for Toney. Danny Kelley, his close friend and workout partner was the first to appear. As his stocky body came towards the striker frame, Toney remembered running eleven miles with Danny just two days before. They pushed each other and drew strength from each other.

As Danny stood over him, a lump formed in Toney's throat. He knew they were headed for the district tournament and he wanted to reach out and slam Danny so bad.

In his usual, easygoing way, Danny said, "Hey man. How's it going?"

"I messed up bad this time."

"You sure did, but you'll be all right."

Toney didn't want Danny to know he was hurt. "I know I will. You better get your running gear ready. We're going to hit the road tomorrow!"

As his voice began to crack, Danny said, "Well, maybe not tomorrow."

As Danny left the room, he knew that he and Toney would not be running tomorrow. He let out a sigh, and wondered if he had lost his teammate forever.

St. Luke's Hospital was near Hermitage and several student nurses were often working. This opened the way for some embarrassing moments.

Toney, paralyzed, unable to feel much of his body, didn't realize that he was naked underneath the sheets. He would lie there, while the nursing students he had grown up with changed his sheets. He didn't know he was exposed.

He finally figured out what the girls were giggling about. He asked that either mama or "older" nurses change his sheets.

Mama and daddy and the girls stayed by Toney's side constantly. There was always somebody there, twenty-four hours a day.

Mama left work and had no plans to return until Toney was better. The doctors told her he would never walk again, but she didn't want to believe it. She kept waiting for someone to tell her different.

She spent all of her time either sleeping, sitting by Toney's side, or praying. She would tell us that the "good Lord will watch over us." It made us all feel better. We all drew strength from her.

One of the most rewarding visits that Toney received was from Coach Donahue and some wrestling teammates. They illegally crowded into his room and made him feel, once again, like he was their leader. They presented him with that same cassette tape box that he was going to buy himself after the district tournament. This time it was chock full of tapes. The wrestlers really made him feel special.

Coach Donahue was always a powerful inspiration to Toney. He pushed him, taught him, and made him work hard in school. He was a big part of Toney's pre-accident life. After a tragedy of such magnitude, you would expect a bond like that to deteriorate. It didn't. Coach Donahue stayed at the hospital like he was a family member. He gave Toney as much support as he always had, but now in a different way. With the help of a man named Bill Carroll, a mutual friend of Toney and the coach, he started the Toney Lineberry Fund to raise money for Toney's future needs. Community support rolled in immediately.

A good friend of Toney's visited him one afternoon. As they talked, Toney expressed concern about his girlfriend. The friend tried to put Toney at ease. "Don't worry about her. I'll take care of her."

Eventually, Toney's girlfriend began spending less time around him. Toney was devastated to learn that she had begun dating the friend who promised to "take care of her."

I suppose it was all just too much for her. She was only sixteen. Their relationship was built around a Toney that didn't exist any more. He would never drive her to school again. He would never carry her on his shoulders again. They would never run through an open field again.

Losing his girl just added to Toney's pain. He was beginning to realize that he had not only been physically injured, he had been emotionally injured. He wondered how a car accident could hurt him so much, in so many ways.

I didn't visit Toney much in those early days. I didn't like seeing him like that and I would become angry. I kept waiting for him to get up and come home. He never did.

It never crossed my mind that he would never walk again. I suppose Toney and I were the only ones who didn't know.

I found out by accident and I wonder to this day if they would have ever told me. We were driving home from the hospital one night after visiting hours. Daddy was driving and Donna and Cathy were in the front seat. I was stretched out in the back seat and had dozed off. I groggily awoke to hear them talking.

One of the girls said "I just can't believe he'll never walk again."

"What are we gonna do?" Daddy replied.

I jumped up and let out a whimper.

"He'll never walk again?"

Tears flowed down my face like a waterfall as I envisioned Toney in a wheelchair, helpless. All I could think was that I had lost my big brother. I felt so empty. I felt like he had died.

I screamed and said it wasn't true and jerked my head around and stared out the back window. Donna climbed into the back seat and hugged me and promised me that Toney and our family would be all right, whether he walked again or not.

I still wouldn't believe it and didn't visit Toney for three or four days.

The big question running through everyone's mind was "what now?" Where would this tragic accident take Toney and our family? Major change was definitely in the works. St. Luke's is a fine hospital, but it was time for Toney to move on to a place that could help him more, a place better equipped to handle spinal cord injury.

Mama and daddy had a decision to make. They could either move their son to a hospital in Richmond, only fifteen minutes from their house, or they could move him to University of Virginia Hospital in Charlottesville, seventy-five miles away. I suppose for some people the decision would be easy: put him in the closest one. For mama and daddy it was not that easy. The main concern was who could do the most for Toney, who had the best facilities. They chose U.VA. for that reason. This would mean daily, long drives for mom and dad. For mom it meant leaving her job. She would be by her boy's side at all costs. She left her career of eleven years at the Bank of Virginia without batting an eye. She was like a programmed machine carrying out a mission to see to

Toney's personal well-being.

Toney was excited about the move. To him, it meant he was going to a better place, a place that would make him better. He still hadn't been told the seriousness of his injury, so he thought the move was another step up the ladder on his way to being able to feel and move his body.

There was still the question whether Toney could even handle the move. There was much apprehension and serious discussion about whether or not it was time for such a bold step. Toney would get frustrated and say "get me out of this place!"

The decision was finally made. Toney would be moved on Friday afternoon. After a week of intense anticipation the day finally arrived. Toney awoke that morning with a gleam in his eyes. He didn't feel his usual morning pain. Mama came in equally excited, and dad, me and my sisters were all set to send him off.

That's when a big blow hit. A man from administration came in. He was only doing his job, I suppose, but in a cold way he told mom and dad, with Toney listening in, that there wasn't a bed available at U.VA., that it would be a few days.

Toney was devastated. He had horrible visions of staying in that awful hospital forever. He cried and looked into mama's eyes. "Why can't I just go home?" She had no answer.

We all felt bad. Even though no real harm was done and the move was merely postponed, we somehow felt defeat. We weren't used to that. We wanted him away from that miserable hospital where we had shed so many tears.

Finally the jubilant day arrived. That Sunday morning was just like the earlier Friday, but this time doctors and nurses were buzzing around trying to get Toney ready for the trip. His body was delicate and had to be handled with care. Mama insisted on helping and bathed him on the striker frame. The frame was a tremendous obstacle and got in the way considerably when they tried to dress him. Clothes had to be cut to get them over the poles. It was January, so no part of his body could be exposed. He wasn't tailor fitted, but the job was done. He was covered.

There seemed like hoards of people surrounding the combination striker frame-stretcher as it rolled down the hall. Family and friends shouted best wishes. Nurses were crying because they had become so attached to this charming, broken eighteen-year-old.

Toney had not been outside in ten days and the air was extremely cold as it knifed through his lungs. But the breeze tracing across his face made him feel like he was coming back to life.

The ambulance had to be rigged to keep the striker frame stable. Toney's neck must not move. The ride began and they drove incredibly fast. Daddy had left fifteen minutes earlier and they passed him in no time. Toney could see the white L.T.D. out of the corner of his eye.

The rescue worker riding in the ambulance with Toney was very uncomforting. He was greasy, with a scraggly beard, and a gold chain swung from his neck in Toney's view. As the ambulance pulled onto I-64 he began to talk.

"Pretty hot car you had, huh?"

Toney, bolted to a striker frame, I.V.'s attached to both arms, only able to see straight up, had trouble mustering a "yes."

"I've won my last five drag races. I used to crash a lot, but I walked away without a scratch. Guess I'm lucky, huh?"

Toney didn't answer. He was in pain and the guy wasn't making him feel any better. Of all the subjects to talk about, he talks about hot cars and how many crashes he'd survived. This was the last thing Toney wanted to hear as he headed for the place he thought would help him survive.

As the ambulance got off at the Charlottesville exit, Toney's discomfort grew worse. Crossing some railroad tracks, a booming pain shot through his head as the tongs that were lodged there moved back and forth. Each stop would move his body forward and fire a telegraph of pain through his neck. He was relieved as the ambulance wheeled into the emergency room area.

By the time Toney was carefully removed from the ambulance we had caught up. I can remember watching as they unloaded him. He looked so uncomfortable. I wasn't used to seeing him like that. I had hardly ever seen him with a headache. Now he looked so pained, so helpless.

We all followed the stretcher as it was wheeled along a hall to a waiting area. We drifted behind Toney, like a boat's wake, waiting to see his new home. We sat in a room and waited, Toney trying to talk to everyone, while his room was being prepared.

Finally someone told us it was ready and we again filed behind the stretcher as it was wheeled into a big, dark, dingy elevator. It moved to the fifth floor and we were led into another waiting room for thirty minutes.

During this wait word got around that the only reason this bed was available for Toney was that its previous occupant had died. It was not a happy thought.

The room was finally ready and Toney was wheeled to the place that would be his home for three months. Quite disturbingly, the room looked a lot like his old room at St. Luke's.

The room was bigger, and had three other patients, all being helped to breathe by respirators. It was dark and quiet, except for the sounds of the respirators: "PPCHCH . . . PPCHCH." There were wooden wheelchairs beside each bed. They looked hard and uncomfortable. The room had a sick smell. It grabbed your nostrils and wouldn't let go. It smelled sterile, awful. It was like all the medicines and ointments in the world mixed together.

I'll never forget that smell.

A tear rolled down Toney's face when he saw the room from the corner of his eye. It was not the paradise, the savior land he had hoped for. It was another dreary hospital intensive care unit.

With the horror of the room just sinking in, another disturbing time arrived. It was time to say goodbye. We each took turns going in to see Toney. We would go in groups of two or three and tell him how much we loved him and how we just knew he'd get better. It was really hard for me, it all seemed so final, so depressingly final. I looked down over him and we both forced a smile.

"I'll be all right buddy," he whispered.

I grabbed his limp hand and said chokingly, "I know you will." I cried hard as I walked out.

The scene continued with everybody getting a small visit. The room was filled with sorrow. We all felt his pain.

The line to visit finally dwindled and mom and dad were the last to see Toney. To say he was upset would be an understatement. He was terrified. He didn't understand why everyone had to leave. Mama promised that they wouldn't be far, but the empty feeling in Toney's stomach remained.

When mom and dad left, a really horrible feeling overcame Toney. He thought he was being left in that awful room to die. He had been told that there were three others in the room but all he could hear were respirators, "PPCHCH . . . PPCHCH."

He thought that was what death sounded like.

After what seemed like hours to Toney a nurse finally arrived. He was horrified and screaming and he asked what that awful noise was.

"It's a respirator. It helps those people breathe."

"Will I need one?"

The nurse seemed genuinely concerned.

"No, you're young and strong. They're older and are hurt worse than you."

This set Toney's mind at ease a little, but he still felt that since he was in that horrible room with those poor people, he must be as bad off as they were.

Toney's three roommates were all in terrible shape. There was an elderly lady who had been brutally beaten by her husband. Since the respirator wouldn't allow her to talk, she would click her teeth to get the nurse's attention.

Another roommate was a man in his mid-thirties. He was a father of two and had severe head and spinal injuries. He had been in an automobile accident. Toney would learn later that fifty percent of all spinal cord injuries are due to auto accidents. Two of the four in that room fit that description.

The last of the roommates was a black, elderly man they called "Pops." Pops was a man that you felt sorry for as soon as you saw him. He was old, but in a "cute" sort of way. He seemed to always have a little smile on his face. He always had trouble as the respirator helped him breathe. It looked like he was always struggling. He had been robbed and beaten for the $3.50 that he had in his pocket.

Pops would beat on the rail of his bed to get the nurse. It seemed like there was always a "click click" from the lady or a "clank clank" from Pops. Toney wondered what it would be like not to be able to talk.

For several days things went well for Toney. Despite the dreariness of the room, he felt okay because there was always someone by his side. Mama and daddy had taken up residence at a Howard Johnson's and were with Toney every second they could be. Me and the girls spent weekends there and I lived with Donna during the week.

I'll never forget one Saturday morning when we were all there. The six of us stood in the waiting room and acted cheerful, like things were looking up.

A doctor came in and shattered us all by saying "It's gonna get worse before it gets better." The words were devastating. I suppose we needed to be prepared, but the hurt at the time made it hard to sink in. Here was our brother, broken, tongs gaping from his head, and this guy tells us it's gonna get worse. I'll never forget the miserable feeling I got in my stomach.

The following Monday morning Toney received the worst news of his life. Some friends were visiting when a young doctor entered the room. He asked everyone to leave so he could talk to Toney alone. The doctor was a stranger to Toney and it scared him. He said that he had bad news but he wanted to give it to him straight.

"You've suffered a broken neck and a severed spinal cord."

Toney was not exactly a medical student and he didn't understand what that meant.

"Well, can you fix it?"

"It's a permanent injury. You'll never walk again or move your fingers."

Toney was crushed. He just couldn't believe it.

He wouldn't believe it. Mama came in and he was hysterical. She smothered him with a hug and promised she'd take care of him. He just cried his eyes out and kept saying "It's not true." No matter how hard he tried, he couldn't move his fingers or legs.

Times were hard. Depression set in for Toney as the inevitable question rolled over and over in his mind. "Why me?" As he would lie in bed listening to the "ppchch ppchchs," the "click clicks," and the "clank clanks," he would remember back when he was strong and healthy, when he was in control of his body, when he could walk. He would feel sorry for himself and think "I can't believe I'll never walk again." He couldn't understand why this had happened to him. There were two thousand kids at his school, why him? He wondered if he would ever figure out why.

As the days went on Toney began to have trouble breathing. Fluid would build up in his lungs and coughing was getting harder every day.

One morning, a typical morning, as mama was feeding Toney some corn flakes, the doctor burst through the door. From his experience with doctors, Toney knew it wasn't good news.

"Stop! Don't feed him those!"

Toney and mama looked in amazement as the doctor continued.

"Toney has developed pneumonia and he can no longer eat solid food. We're gonna have to put him on the respirator!"

Toney was terrified. He would now be like the other three, broken and quiet. He already couldn't move, but now he wouldn't be able to talk or eat either. That last bit of corn flakes was his last bite of solid food for two months. He sunk lower than he had ever been before.

Pneumonia is common among spinal cord injured patients. Lying on one's back so often causes fluids and phlegm to build up in their lungs. The only way to clear it is to perform a tracheotomy, cutting an incision in the wind pipe, sticking in a tube, and suctioning. The recovery is long and drawn out, and while the windpipe is open, a respirator must take over its job. "PPCHCH . . . PPCHCH."

Toney would now develop a strong bond with Pops. They were one and the same. They would give each other looks, sometimes a smile but usually a grimace, when they were positioned to see each other. They would stare into each other's mind as they shared a common bond, a bond of pain.

The respirator made life very hard for Toney. First, he was unable to eat. It's not so much that he was craving for food all the time, but that he began to lose large amounts of weight. He went from his big, solid, wrestling frame to a puny 103 pounds. Starvation became a threat, and another painful tube was worked down his nose to feed nutrients.

Above not being able to eat was the awful handicap of not being able to talk. Communicating became a problem. Reading lips is not something many people are able to do. Mama became good at it. She was sort of his translator for everyone. Quite often, though, the message wouldn't get through. No one could tell what he wanted. He would get frustrated, feeling defeated. He had a horrible fear that his voice would never return. He couldn't stand the thought of that.

Toney's pneumonia got worse and worse. Some nights were really bad. One cold February night, fluid was building up in his chest so bad that even the respirator was having a hard time making him breathe. Mama and Coach Donahue took turns pushing on his stomach to get the air through. It was a long night and mama later said that she really feared he would die that night. It was as if she was fighting death with every pump of his chest.

Nights were rough, dark and lonely. If Toney was doing okay, mama would go to the hotel room and get some sleep.

One night Toney was getting along all right and was left alone. Four respirators pumped, one after the other, "PPCHCH . . . PPCHCH . . . PPCHCH . . . PPCHCH."

Suddenly, the number was reduced to three. Blue lights were flashing and a cardiogram was buzzing one solid beep. Doctors and nurses were making a limp body jump with massive voltage.

It was no use. Pops was dead. As a nurse pulled a sheet over his face, Toney screamed as hard as he could, but nothing would come out. Silent tears rolled down his face and he trembled all over. Was he next?

CHAPTER 4
THE STRUGGLE CONTINUES

*L*ightning flashed outside the fifth floor window of the University of Virginia intensive care unit. Rain raced down the sill like it was running for its life. The wind seemed to growl as it ripped through trees and made them bow and creak. Swooshes of water spanked the window pane. The wind pecked at the window in an evil way. The condition outside was mean and frightening, but it was nothing compared to the sheer horror that lurked inside the I.C.U.

As the lightning snapped and the thunder roared, Toney's ears would ache. With every boom of thunder he saw himself smashing into the dash. Every flash of lightning brought the ambulances, coming to rescue him. He had awful nightmares about the accident every night as he slept, but this time he was reliving the hideous event as he lay awake. Every click, click of the lady in the next bed brought horrible visions of his bloody, moaning friend drooped over the seat. He screamed but nothing came out. The lights were off and he desperately wanted them on.

"Oh God," he silently mouthed, "help me."

Storms were hard on the intensive care unit. Electricity is taken for granted until it's gone. The people in the I.C.U. had to have it to live. Backup generators would cut in but it would take a minute. When electric machines are helping you breathe, that's a minute you don't have.

When the electricity goes out someone has to be there to operate a hand "pump" to keep the patient breathing.

On a stormy night it was common for mama or one of our sisters to sit up with that pump in hand throughout the night.

On this night Cathy sat and frantically pumped air into her

brother's lungs. The minute it took for the generator to cut in seemed like hours to Cathy. She was afraid Toney would die.

A stormy night is hard on the I.C.U.

Mom and dad's home for that winter was Howard Johnson's, a nice little motel but not comfortable for a long period of time. That little room with its little view got old. The motel restaurant food got old. Life for the parents of a broken eighteen-year-old was getting old.

Charlottesville, nestled in the Blue Ridge Mountains, is a pretty town. From the beautiful architecture of Thomas Jefferson to the rolling terrain. It really is a nice place. But like all nice places, bad things still happen there. My family, especially my brother, lived through hell in that nice little town.

My sisters and I would visit on weekends. Me, Donna, Mike and little Mike made the seventy-five minute drive every Friday. That patch of interstate 64 got old, but we never stopped going. The doctors had told us that Toney needed support and we were going to make sure he got it.

Terry would leave work early and Cathy would skip an occasional Friday class at James Madison University for an extra day to visit with their brother. They were even glad to see me on weekends. We talked to each other and hugged each other more than we ever had. It's ironic that it was such a horrible situation that brought our family so close together.

Visits with Toney were common for all of us. Some were spent laughing, some were spent crying. Some were spent just sitting by a sleeping Toney, wondering and thinking of things that might have been.

Visits took one of two paths. If Toney's striker frame had him flipped on his back, it would be the usual "sit in a chair" visit. If the frame had him flipped on his stomach, we would have to lie on our back underneath Toney.

Quite often Cathy would come see Toney with a tape player. She would lie under the frame, a pillow under her head, and sing to the tapes the wrestling team had given him. Toney would sing along, just moving his lips.

These were great moments for Toney. It was a time to laugh, a time to forget his troubles and enter the world that the particular song was presenting.

All too soon, however, the tape would click off. A nurse would tell Cathy it's time to leave and reality would set in. They would both cry as she left him.

I had trouble visiting Toney. I didn't know what to say and I felt scared and uncomfortable. I would always go in to see him but I wouldn't stay as long as the others. At twelve, it was hard for me to look at him. He just didn't look the same. He was my big brother, the person I looked up to more than anybody in the world. Now all he could do was suffer in that bed. I wanted him to hit me up side my head, to do something, so bad.

I remember sitting in that awful U.VA. waiting room fighting back tears. Remember, a twelve-year-old boy isn't supposed to cry. I sat there with a terrible feeling. I felt like I wasn't supporting Toney enough. I felt like I wasn't there as much as the girls were. I wanted to help, I really did. But what could I do or say to help my brother?

Finally it came to me. It was time to leave and everyone took their turn to say goodbye. I waited to be last and I pulled a chair over to the striker frame. I jumped up in it so I could see Toney over the rails of the frame. My eyes began to water. I felt a big cry coming on and I gritted my teeth trying to hold it back. Fighting those tears was one of the hardest things I've ever had to do, but I had to do it. I leaned over the bed and whispered the three simple words "I love you." The inevitable tears began to flow and they dripped on Toney's face as he mouthed back "I love you too, buddy." I jumped down off the chair and ran out of the room crying as hard as I ever had before. Donna squeezed me in the hall and the tears continued to flow. I couldn't stop crying, but I hadn't felt that good in a month.

It was the first time we ever said we loved each other.

Toney's striker frame was very, very painful. That's why it was such a great day when the doctors said he was strong enough to be freed from it. It would mean that those grotesque tongs could be taken from his head and those ton-like thirty pound weights that had been pulling at his neck for so long could be removed.

The only bad part was that getting this done meant another grueling trip to the operating room. Extreme caution would have to be taken since a machine was making Toney breathe.

Being taken off the striker frame is not as simple as it sounds. There is a very complex operation that must be performed. When there is a broken neck, the bone is snapped in two. In order for the neck to be held up and used again the bone must be fused back together.

When the operation begins there is no turning back. Bone chips, from a hip, are taken and solution is added to form a pasty substance. This substance is filled with wire to make what will eventually be part of the neck bone. An eight-inch incision is cut in the neck at the place of the break and the neck is fused back together.

The neck was back together, but the fusion meant nothing to Toney. The spinal cord is a bundle of nerves that act as a telephone line from the brain to the body. The vertebra can be fused back together, but the nerves cannot be. They are destroyed, which means permanent paralysis.

Nevertheless, Toney was now off the striker frame and was able to "enjoy" a real hospital bed. For the first time since his accident he was able to actually sit up. There was a large, ugly, skin-colored brace around his neck. It had a hole in it so the respirator hose could enter his throat. Tubes were still jutting from his body and there were ugly scabs on his head where the tongs that had held him to the frame had been. He wasn't a pretty sight, but he somehow looked more alive away from that striker frame.

Although Toney was off the striker frame there was still one menacing piece of machinery that he relied on desperately. "PPCHCH . . . PPCHCH," it sat beside his bed and made that awful sound.

Toney would lie there and wonder if he would ever breathe on his own again.

He was sick of being fed through tubes and he was sick of not being able to talk, or able to scream. He was terrified that for the rest of his life he would have to lie in bed with tubes coming out of him like an octopus.

He had awful thoughts of his voice never coming back, of having to learn sign language or having to go "click click" so his mama would come to his bed. He wondered if he would have to mouth everything he said and just hope the world understood.

Toney was able to sit up for a few hours a day, but the majority of his time was spent lying flat on his back. Imagine lying on your back twenty-two hours a day. Even if you weren't fighting for your life, it would be tough.

Toney would lie on his back just waiting, hoping for the day to end. Anytime he could sleep it was welcome. It meant ticks of the clock had gone by. Each tick meant, in his mind, that he was closer to getting better.

He watched lots of television, but that got old. You can only watch so many reruns without losing your mind.

Sometimes he would lie for hours and count the dots on the ceiling or the lines on the wallpaper.

Sometimes he would just think. And remember.

* * * * *

The runner from Fairfield was a half-inch in front of him. The finish line was a hundred yards away. Little Lineberry, the Brookland runner in the quarter mile, was running his hardest trying to beat the kid. It was as if they were both running in slow motion as they approached the tape neck-and-neck. Feet were pulsing, arms pumping, torsos were leaning, stretching, and reaching.

Five feet to go, the crowd was screaming and a coach named Samuels was jumping up and down in a blue sweat suit, squeezing a stopwatch.

Toney lunged into the cinders, across the finish line and inched out the Fairfield runner by a head. Third place was his.

With blood dripping from his knee, Toney received a yellow

ribbon and a pat on the back from Coach Samuels. He had given up his body to get third place for his team.

* * * * *

Toney was startled when the nurse rolled him on his side, interrupting his heroic daydream. It was back to the real world of pain.

If Toney wasn't sleeping, thinking, or remembering, there was a nurse or doctor by his bed. It's hard to be around nurses and doctors all the time. Someone in Toney's condition is used to lots of pity and attention. Nurses and doctors can't give that all the time. They see hundreds of patients a day and they just can't feel sorry for all of them all of the time.

Nurses and doctors are people, too. They have good days and bad days. Sometimes the compassion that makes them so great at what they do isn't obvious. The patient sometimes doesn't realize this and is bitter towards them. However, the patient needs the nurse or doctor, and the nurse or doctor truly wants to help the patient.

Quite often a physical therapist would roll Toney on his side and start giving him karate chops to the back. To Toney it was torture, but it was a necessary thing. The chops helped loosen the phlegm in his chest that was clogging up his lungs.

With the respirator going full blast a nurse would come at Toney with a tube, ready to stick it down his throat. To Toney she had an evil look in her eye, but she was only preparing to suction the phlegm that had come loose.

Doctors frightened Toney. They were always tall, with a clip board in their hand. And they never smiled. They would just read the clipboard, whisper to a nurse, and slowly walk out with their white jacket waving in the air. Toney hated seeing them and didn't want them around him. It's ironic that they were the reason he was alive.

Toney was getting very tired of not being able to breathe on his own. He felt like he might be able to take a breath now and then, but every time he tried the machine would take over. "PPCHCH

. . . PPCHCH." Toney hated that sound so much. He started feeling like he was a machine. He felt like a wrestler who couldn't wrestle, a runner who couldn't run, a person who had become a machine.

It was obvious that Toney was getting stronger. He was spunky with the nurses and he mouthed more to us. He stayed awake longer and wanted music and action more. He desperately wanted to at least partially function as a human.

One Sunday, a typical Sunday, with mom, dad, me and my sisters huddled around Toney's bed, a doctor entered. Toney began to frown. He wasn't expecting good news.

"We've decided to try and remove you from the respirator. It appears that you have built up enough strength in your lungs to breathe on your own again."

Toney popped his lips in excitement as we all hugged him. Finally something good had happened.

I had a tremendous feeling of relief. I finally lost that awful fear that my brother might die.

The doctor warned us that it may not be successful and it would be a long, drawn out process. We didn't care, his words going in one ear and out the other. It was another step in Toney's recovery, a sign of better things to come.

Much to our (and especially Toney's) dismay, the doctors put off removing him from the respirator for days. They said they were letting as much strength build up as possible. Toney didn't care. He wanted "off that stupid machine now!"

The jubilant day arrived. We all wanted to be in the room, but only mama and daddy were allowed.

After careful instructions for Toney to try and breathe calmly and slowly, the doctor unhooked the tube and cut the machine off. With a smile, Toney drew in several breaths of wrinkled, tired, puny, human air. The sixth one came harder and the doctors hooked the machine back up.

Toney, mama, and daddy had a look of disgust, but the doctors were pleased. It was a good start.

Toney was mad as hell that he couldn't just start breathing on his own right away. But he came to realize that it had to be done and he felt better and better as he could breathe longer and longer each time the machine was cut off. It would be months before it was off forever, but Toney felt good that he was a living, breathing human being again, even part of the time.

With a few breaths of air coming his way, another test was put before Toney. It was time to try to talk. As the doctor put his finger over the tube he asked Toney to try to say something. He had only the strength to say one word. In a squeaky, very high voice he mustered "mama."

Everyone was so happy. Toney would talk as long as his breath would let him. The nurses would tell him to shut up so he could breathe longer. It was no use, he had too much to say. "Remember that day I tried to tell you my nose itched. I moved my lips for three hours!"

Toney's worst fear was now but a nightmare. He had his voice back, a tool that shouldn't be taken for granted. He now waited for other parts of his body to come back to use. It would be a long wait.

The days seemed to grow a bit shorter. Toney was breathing most of the time, an oxygen tank right beside his bed for the twenty-five percent of the time he wasn't.

Toney constantly wondered when his throat would be able to swallow food. It, too had grown weak and needed time to recuperate. The doctors waited a very long time for this. Choking would be a major setback, and no one wanted that.

On a sunny afternoon the tall, well-groomed doctor entered.
"How do you feel, Toney?"
"Good," Toney replied in a high but no longer squeaky voice.
"We're thinking you might be able to handle some solid food."
Toney beamed. His smile seemed as wide as the Grand Canyon as visions of a big steak and baked potatoes danced in his head.

We all made sure we were at the hospital on this day, mama and daddy, my sisters and me, and Coach Donahue. Toney's first meal was on its way up, and we weren't going to miss that.

Finally a doctor escorted the tray in. When a nurse lifted the food cover Toney's face drooped. There, on that ugly, blue cafeteria tray, was a little clump of orange jello and what looked like a specimen glass full of orange juice.

It was no steak and baked potatoe, but it was better than nothing. With mama working the fork, Toney savored every drop. We all clapped as a piece of jello dripped out the corner of his mouth.

Toney's first "real" meal came the next week, on Monday. Everyone, except mama and daddy, had gone back to their regular weekday life. It was a dark, quiet day. Two awful respirators were still pumping alongside other beds. The doctor had said Toney could eat something a bit more solid and a tray was on the way up.

An old cafeteria woman, with her hair in a bun, slowly rolled a cart towards Toney's bed. She sat his tray on a table as mama and daddy watched.

Mama opened the food cover and a triangular shape formed over Toney's lips.

"What is it?" Toney whimpered.

Mama finally surmised that it was a burnt grilled cheese sandwich.

Toney pleaded, "Please don't make me eat it!"

Mama and daddy were not about to make him eat that sandwich. They replied in unison "What do you want?"

Toney was as excited as a rat at the dump.

"A B.L.T., an order of fries, and a Mountain Dew!" He had been dying for a Mountain Dew for three months. It was always his favorite soft drink.

Before the words "Mountain Dew" came out daddy was on his way to the diner.

When the gourmet meal came back Toney ate it all. He was about ready to bite mama's fingers as she fed him the last bite.

It was the best meal he'd ever had in his life.

It was a prescription for happiness. It was like a dark cloud had been lifted from over his bed. He joked again. Mama and daddy leaned over his bed and grinned. They would be with him for the rest of his life. He would never go hungry and would never go without love.

Toney began to eat more and more. The hospital food was rarely good enough and it seemed as though someone was always scampering off towards a restaurant.

I remember one day Toney had to have a Western Sizzlin' steak and Coach Donahue and I drove all over Charlottesville looking for one.

The fact that Toney could eat was great, but there was still one thing bothering us all. He had to be fed and it was awkward and sometimes didn't go well. Mama did the feeding, but others sometimes took over.

Not being able to pick up his arms and feed himself really bothered Toney. He couldn't stand the thought of not being able to do something so basic. The excitement of being able to eat wore off and he began skipping meals so no one would have to feed him.

We all wanted to feed Toney. We loved the idea of doing something for him.

On one frosty, Sunday afternoon Toney was especially hungry. Terry was excited. She was about to feed him for the first time.

It was not something she was good at. She would cram the food in his mouth like he was a kid and he would have to tell her to slow down.

Terry was really trying hard but was having a rough time.

The real obstacle hit when she came to the peas. They kept falling off the fork and Toney would get one out of ten. Terry became frustrated and threw the fork down. She stomped out of the room crying.

Daddy couldn't feed Toney at all. He tried but would choke up. It hurt him that his once strong son couldn't do little things. He would take long walks around Charlottesville so his tears wouldn't show up in front of Toney.

Eventually more and more tubes and wires were being unhooked from Toney. He began looking less and less like a spider web.

Easter hit and more evidence of how much support Toney had rolled in. His bed was surrounded by dozens of Easter baskets with candy gushing out of each one. Cards lined the walls and piled up on tables. His mail was like a movie star's and we all helped opening things.

I especially liked taking care of the baskets and that candy.

Toney made lots of friends with those baskets. When a nurse or attendant would walk by he'd tell them to fill their pockets.

Times were getting better. Toney was getting stronger. It seemed as though life was getting a bit more normal. Some days were even filled with cheer. Some days even went by fast. Some days the television reruns were good and the food went down well. Some days not one single tear would be shed.

On other days Toney couldn't breathe. An oxygen mask would cover his nose and mouth and his eyes would shoot sadness at you. Some days all Toney could think about was a mangled Mustang, an icy road, or heaven. Some days had no consequence at all. They would be marked off the calendar as insignificant, unproductive days. Depression would set in quite often and Toney would have "why me" days. He would lie there and hate the world and wish he was home.

Weekends perked things up. Toney would be bombarded by visitors, never fail.

One Saturday afternoon Toney decided he didn't want to just sit by the bed for his "hour up" that day. He asked if he could be rolled around. His oxygen tank was set up to be carted with him.

Our sister Donna pushed him down the hall in an old wooden, rickety wheelchair.

He rolled past other patients and couldn't stand seeing them. They looked awful.

He rolled past a flight of stairs and wondered what someone in a wheelchair was supposed to do.

He rolled past a window and saw the Towers Rehabilitation Hospital across the street. He hoped to someday be there.

As the chair creaked along Toney saw, up ahead, something he hadn't seen in a while, a mirror. He asked Donna to roll him to it and he wished he could comb his hair.

When they got to the mirror it was not filled with what Toney expected. There, in that mirror, he didn't see a 119 pound block of steel. Instead a pale, boney, ninety-eight pound shell stared back. He was gaunt and weak looking. There were two brown, rusty scars on his forehead. There was a big hole in his throat. And there were no muscles.

Toney cried, then screamed, "That's not me!"

CHAPTER 5
WHY ME?

"*Why me?*" "*Why me?*" *It was as if there was a big neon sign flashing in Toney's mind. There were two thousand kids at his school, billions of people in the world. Why him?! He knew there must be an answer, but he couldn't think of it. He spent hours and hours searching for it, but he couldn't find it.*

Toney began sitting up more and more each day. He began needing oxygen less and less. Instead of lying in bed thinking, he would sit in that chair with wheels and think. He thought about lots of things, his family, his past, his condition.

Mostly he thought about what the rest of his life would be like. He thought about the doctor telling him something about a severed spinal cord and how he would never walk again. He must have had some sort of mental block because that just wouldn't sink in. "There's no way. I'll walk again. I'm too strong. I'll just have to work hard, that's all."

Toney knew that somewhere out there was something, somebody, or some place that could help him. He was not a quitter, and he decided that he would fight until he could feel and move his "dead" legs.

"I know somebody can help me."

As time passed it became more and more apparent that there wasn't much more U.VA. Hospital could do for Toney. For a while they kept him alive. He couldn't have made it without them. But it was time to take a step towards rehabilitation. To Toney, rehabilitation meant getting better.

That wonderful rehabilitation was right across the street at a place called Towers Hospital. Towers is a tall, brick building that looks more like a hotel than a hospital. In that building Toney saw hope. That was the place that would make him better.

You could hear mama's voice ringing through the receiver as she called us at Donna and Mike's house.

"Toney's getting out of the hospital!"

Everyone was very happy. I had visions of my big brother coming home.

The excitement died down a little when mama told us he was going to another hospital.

The move to Towers really was something to whistle about. It meant Toney was out of the woods, that he would survive. He was going to a place that could help him more. There was a chance for progress, a chance to get out of that awful intensive care unit and actually become a functioning person.

Towers wasn't a place to sit and wait. It was a place to learn, a place to help you move on with your life. To Toney it was the promised land, a workshop for miracles.

It was the beginning of spring when Toney was told he would be moved to Towers. Grass was growing, buds were forming on trees, flowers were sprouting, kids seemed to again be scampering about. Everything was coming back to life as he was freed from that fifth floor intensive care unit. There would be no more "PPCHCH . . . PPCHCH." Machines would no longer dominate his day. Life, once again, pumped from Toney's lungs.

Moving Toney was like a major construction job. His body had barely been moved around the halls in months, much less outside. The doctors checked him over from head to toe before they okayed his release. There would have to be absolutely no reason for him to stay in intensive care before he could be moved.

The exam was positive. The doctors warned that his breathing was not yet 100 percent and oxygen should always be near. They wished him luck and sent him on his way.

After Toney was bundled up to protect his sensitive, indoor-ridden skin, he was lifted onto a stretcher and rolled into the hall, away from the I.C.U., for the last time.

He was again surrounded by family and friends as he was

rolled towards the elevator.

As Toney was being loaded into that same big, black elevator that he was brought up on, a few U.VA. nurses cried as they waved. I thought they were just gonna miss his Easter candy. Instead, they would miss Toney. He was the cute, broken eighteen-year-old that they had seen through so many hard times.

An ambulance was waiting outside the hospital. As the doors of the building opened, sadness seemed to float out of them. We were glad to be leaving that depressing atmosphere.

Toney was carefully loaded into the ambulance. It's twin doors closed at the same time the doors of the hospital closed. As Toney was locked in the ambulance, the sadness seemed locked in the building. Unfortunately, the sadness was of a generic nature. It would lurk in other hospitals to come.

The ambulance made the "journey" across the street. We waited on the curb as Toney was unloaded in the Towers parking lot. The sun glared down on the stretcher and in Toney's eyes. He squinted as he searched for a familiar face.

We all huddled around Toney's stretcher. We talked and laughed. We couldn't wait to get inside and see Toney's new home.

"This place looks nice."

"They should really help him here!"

Optimism floated in the air.

Coming across the parking lot there was a loud noise that turned everyone's head. There, rolling down the curb of the Towers sidewalk, was a wheelchair being pushed by a man in white. The chair needed oiling, but it looked good. It had sort of a personality to it, rubber wheels, vinyl armrests, metal foot plates, and even a vinyl back rest. It looked half-comfortable, unlike the wooden chairs at U.VA.

The chair was Toney's. It was on loan from the hospital and would be his until mama and daddy could order one. That chair, or one like it, would be Toney's means of transportation forever. It would be where he would sit for the rest of his life.

Apprehension set in as Toney was wheeled through the big,

electric doors at Towers. The first floor was sort of a lobby, with plants and nice furniture everywhere. There was an admitting desk with a smiling nurse behind it. There were people actually walking around the hospital smiling! Toney began to grow suspicious as the pain in his neck told him this place couldn't be all smiles.

When Toney got off at the second floor he was shocked. There seemed to be a color about the place. The attendant told him this was his floor and his room was just down the hall.

Before they went to his room the attendant pushed Toney into the recreation room. Inside, Toney couldn't believe his eyes.

There were lots of tables, with few chairs. There was a water fountain at wheelchair's height and pool tables and ping-pong tables just as low. The windows were at chair's height. It was a recreation room for people who couldn't walk.

These things really shocked Toney. But he was most shaken by all the people in wheelchairs in one place. They would just roll around, some of them even laughing, in that room. Toney could see himself blending in with them and he hated the thought. All of a sudden his new chair was not as modern as he thought. He couldn't stand the idea of living in a place like this.

Tears rolled down his face and mama held his limp hand as he was rolled towards his room. "You won't be here long, honey. They'll really help you."

Toney's room was a double with one side empty. He had the side next to the window and one side of his bed was lined with emergency oxygen tanks. The room was plain, but mama and the girls promised color would arrive soon.

Toney stared out of the handicap height window into the clouds. There, as if the clouds were a television screen, he saw our room in Laurel Park. His bed was in a corner, his stereo beside it. Posters were on the wall and the Hermitage wrestling schedule was pinned on the bulletin board. He saw himself bouncing out of bed after the D.J. announced school would be closed because of snow.

"Toney." A woman put her hand on Toney's shoulder and

awoke him from his daydream. His frown slumped deeper as she spoke.

"I'm Paula. Welcome to Towers! I'll be your therapist here. We'll start tomorrow. Okay?"

Paula was small, thin and attractive. Toney wondered how the petite, young therapist would be able to lift him in and out of his wheelchair. Paula knew how to use her weight, however, and this would not be a problem.

It was horrible for us to leave Toney that night. He seemed as sad as I'd ever seen him, and I'd seen him at the bottom during the last three months. He wanted to go home with us so bad. If I could have gotten away with it I would have smuggled him home in the trunk of our car. At that moment, he didn't care about therapy or getting better. He just wanted to go home.

When visitors hours forced us away we left Toney for his first night at Towers. He was alone for the first time but would be monitored constantly.

He couldn't sleep. He lie in his dark, lonely room with an awful thought. Was this place really just a nursing home and not a rehabilitation hospital at all? Was this his new, permanent home? His body trembled as he cried and wished mama was there. He stared at the empty wheelchair beside his bed. "Why me?"

Progress was slow for Toney. It was a big day when he could lift his arms to chin level. For the first week and a half that's what therapy was, lifting his arms.

His injury left him with biceps, but no triceps. He could lift to curl, but he couldn't straighten his arm out to point to a wall. His fingers were completely paralyzed and it was not yet clear whether he would ever be able to move his wrists.

Everyday was a struggle. Paula coached Toney along and taught him things day by day. He was getting to the point where he had some coordination in his arms.

It was always the hospital's policy to encourage patients to eat meals with their peers. One morning Paula decided it was time for Toney to eat in the cafeteria, and feed himself breakfast. Toney was scared, but nodded his head as Paula helped him into his chair.

The cafeteria was crowded that morning. The room was full of handicapped people, talking and eating, preparing for a day of rehabilitation.

As Toney looked with disgust at the runny eggs on his plate, Paula cut up his sausage and biscuit and put the fork in his hand. After all Toney had accomplished in his life — football championships, wrestling titles, track ribbons — suddenly the most difficult thing he had to do was get a piece of that sausage on that fork.

His skinny arm tried desperately to stab a piece of sausage, but it would only slide around the plate. He couldn't draw enough strength in his arm to puncture the piece of pork. He once bench pressed 250 pounds.

Suddenly his arm cooperated and a little piece of sausage clung futilely to the fork. In almost a triumphant manner Toney raised the fork ten inches. Just as it was about to reach his hungry mouth, the sausage fell in his lap. In a burst of anger Toney slammed the fork on his plate. "The hell with it!"

Toney and Paula had developed a strong bond and she wouldn't let him give up. "If you want to eat you have to feed yourself."

Toney couldn't believe she wasn't going to feed him. "Can't she see I can't do it?" he thought.

"I can't do it." Toney had never said that before in his life. He said it on this day, with a growling stomach and tears in his eyes.

Without asking, Paula put the fork back in Toney's hand and gave him a small smile. Quietly, he tried, and tried to get the sausage on the fork. The morning moved on, new diners came in and out, Toney tried some more.

Finally, with the care of a surgeon, he got a piece into his mouth. It was the best sausage he had ever had. Many more pieces would fall in his lap, but the breakfast would be eaten. Toney smiled. It was the first independent thing that the handicapped Toney had ever done.

It was obvious that Toney would have limited use of his arms. It was therefore very important to completely build up what he had left. This meant therapy, and more therapy.

Therapy was on the first floor. Many a weight had been lifted there. Toney would sit in the room just lifting his arms. Up and down, up and down, it was like he was giving sign language but only knew one sign.

* * * * *

"Hey Lineberry, put my machine on 200!" Lineberry slammed down his 100 pound curl and put his teammate's bench press on 200. The room reeked with wrestlers. Coach Donahue stood over a lifter. "Push it, push it, keep lifting, keep lifting!"

* * * * *

"Keep lifting, Toney." Paula startled Toney. She had noticed he had stopped lifting his arms. "Only fifteen more minutes until lunch."

* * * * *

An echo haunted Toney. "No lunch today, Lineberry! You've got seven pounds to lose. Better start running!"

* * * * *

Toney always rested at lunch. His body had sat up more the past few weeks than it had in three months. He welcomed those afternoon naps. Sleep was something he had become very used to.

As Toney awoke from one of his afternoon naps, he saw an attendant pushing a very scared person in a wheelchair through the door. He reminded Toney of himself.

The boy's name was Hugh. His black hair was scrambled in every direction and he had a wild look in his eyes. He looked like he hadn't shaven in months. His body was frail, even frailer than Toney's, and his clothes were dirty and wrinkled.

Toney noticed that the boy had no family with him, no friends. Toney sighed and wondered what had happened to the poor fellow.

Hugh was a wanderer, hitchhiking up and down the East Coast for the last five of his twenty-four years. His legs were his only asset, and he lost them when a guy he was hitchhiking with swerved off a cliff. Now he would spend the rest of his life in state-run hospitals.

He gave the nurses and attendants a hard time, constantly playing like he was dying or calling them names. On most any day you could hear his crackly voice yell to an attendant passing by. "Heeeey monkey face!"

Hugh was desperate for love. He adopted our family. We spent time with him and made him feel like he was part of our family. We got him through many days.

He got us through many days, too. He seemed to always bring laughter into rotten situations. I remember having to leave the floor because my laughter would disturb other patients. Toney would often need oxygen because he was laughing so hard.

The days got shorter for Toney and he began to be able to do more and more with his arms. He moved up to wrist weights when lifting his arms. At times he felt half good, like progress was being made. He would have optimistic thoughts and dream of the pot of gold at the end of his rehabilitation rainbow.

More often, though, he would lift the weights and think of it only as torture. His dreams were only of things that might have been.

Some injuries weren't as severe as others. Toney's was one of the worst and he had to watch in many rehabilitative activities.

Some spinal cord injuries aren't complete. Instead of being severed, the cord is bruised or cut. Feeling sometimes comes back with these injuries and rehabilitation is needed to regain as much mobility as possible. There was a walking machine, sort of a treadmill, that some of the patients used to get the strength back in their legs. Toney would watch the patients on the machine and decide that he would do that someday. He didn't care that the doctors said his spinal cord was severed and that there was no way he would ever walk again. He thought if he believed, or wished, hard enough he would be okay. He just knew he would be on that "walking machine" in a month or so.

Occupational therapy, although equally important, was different from physical therapy. O.T. consisted of a wider variety of activities than rebuilding physical strength. The paralyzed person must relearn movement skills. Everything from brushing his teeth to writing. He was in first grade again, an eighteen-year-old baby. It is incredibly frustrating when your mind knows how to do something but your body does not. "Work, you stupid fingers!"

Paula and the Tower's staff were a great help. They knew every little trick and gadget to help the paralyzed person be able to do things you wouldn't think possible for them to do. Their ammunition ranged from cuffs for holding hair brushes and the like, to light switches that you blow on to turn on and off. The handicapped world is a world of gadgets and compromises. Quite often the simplest tasks take engineering marvels to overcome.

Perhaps the most awful loss with spinal cord injury is the loss of bowel and bladder control. The bladder cannot tell the brain it is full. The handicapped person can't just run to the bathroom. These things must be taken care of and controlled by artificial means. To be honest, embarrassing situations are common to the spinal cord injured person. Imagine having to leave a restaurant in mid-meal because you notice your pants are wet.

When people hear of a person becoming spinal cord injured they feel bad about it. They think of all the things he could have accomplished and what he's going to have to go through. The feeling is always "boy is his life going to change." What many people overlook is that not only does his life change, but so do the lives of people around him.

My family has had two lives. We each had a life before Toney's injury. And a different life after it.

My parents became unofficial citizens of Charlottesville. Their jobs were second and their boy was first. Nothing else mattered but his well being. Not only did Toney endure therapy, but so did my parents. Mama underwent countless hours of classes to learn to take care of him. She learned to dress him and to bathe him. She learned to control his bowel and bladder. She would have to learn to be mentally tough. She made the trip to Charlottesville every night to sharpen those skills.

We all attended classes to learn what to expect from life with a person in a wheelchair. Quite often I didn't listen — that wasn't my brother they were talking about.

My life took a turn in those days. I was a seventh grader at Brookland. I was on the wrestling team but I became disinterested. I didn't care about it anymore. I didn't run home from school and play like other junior high students, I went to my sister's house and waited to go to Charlottesville. I don't know how I made it through that. I suppose being so naive about the situation made it easier. I didn't care about much in those days. I became good at being in unhappy scenery. We all did. It became part of our lives. That icy January night changed us forever.

Days became incredibly routine for Toney. Breakfast, therapy, rest, lunch, more therapy, more rest, dinner.

Nights tended to have some variety. The hospital tried very hard to offer plenty of recreation. Some patients had no family and the rec-room was all they had. Toney couldn't play ping-pong or pool like some, but he became very good at card games. He mastered backgammon. It felt good to be able to compete again. Somehow, though, trumping an ace wasn't quite as exciting as pinning a wrestler.

Toney was tutored for high school every day. There were strong hopes of maybe getting his diploma someday. He just went through the motions and didn't put much effort into his studies. He never cared about school before. Why in the world should he care about it now?

There were lots of very big reasons why Toney should care now. Church groups, P.T.A.'s and other organizations poured in support for Toney. Coach Donahue's "Toney Lineberry Fund" had raised $14,000. Many wonderful people made donations in hopes of someday buying a van for Toney.

The coach worked very hard. He organized an event that would be a big lift for Toney. The event was called "Run For Toney." Coach Donahue and seven cross-country runners from Hermitage took pledges and ran from Richmond to Charlottesville. That fifty mile run raised $1,600.00 for the fund.

Coach Donahue presented Toney and my family with "Run For Toney" T-shirts in the Towers parking lot. Toney hugged the coach and told him how much he meant to him.

Toney was beginning to realize how much people cared for him and what they were willing to do for him. He decided he couldn't, and wouldn't, let them down. From that moment on he would give it everything he had.

Toney worked hard in therapy. He wasn't about to let us down. Some people had no reason — and no one — to work hard for. Toney did.

Toney's hair began to grow long and shaggy.

Toney and I have had only one barber our entire life. He is Jimmy Griffith, owner of Jimmy's Barber Shop in Ashland, Virginia. Toney remembered daddy taking us to Jimmy's for crew cuts when we were small. He remembered getting his hair cut the day before his eighteenth birthday.

One afternoon, as Toney's hair drooped into his eyes, Jimmy came smiling through the door of his room. He had a tray of barber's tools in his hand. He really gave Toney a lift as he cut away some of the hair that had grown during these last few months.

Visits always gave Toney a lift. There was a big picture-glass window in the therapy room. On many an afternoon daddy would walk by the window on his way in to see Toney. He'd sit for hours during therapy. Toney would look around, and notice no other patients having visitors. A small smile would form across his lips. He would grit his teeth and try to show daddy some of the old, determined, weight lifting Toney.

Tower's food was horrid. Toney would quite often go hungry if forced to eat it. More often than not, mama and daddy would bring him something. Almost every afternoon, daddy would walk by the therapy room window and, with a grin, hold up a white bag. Toney would smile back, knowing the bag had something good to eat in it.

Not a day went by that Toney didn't think of home. He longed for Laurel Park. He longed to get back to that wonderful place where he grew up. He couldn't remember a single unhappy time that he spent there. He, of course, had some, but they all somehow slipped his mind now. He felt terrible about the situation he was in now, but he thought if he could just go home everything would be fine.

Every time he saw a doctor, he asked when he might be able to go home. Each time they dodged his question.

Finally, on a glorious afternoon, he was told he'd be able to go home for the weekend. It was felt that mama was ready to take care of him and Towers was only needed for rehabilitation.

News of Toney's homecoming traveled fast. We were all ecstatic about it. We were determined that we would make his visit as happy as could be.

Mama and daddy went to get Toney on a Friday afternoon. The therapist said that he had worked especially hard that day, with a gleam in his eye. The mere thought of going home made him improve.

Even on this day mama and daddy would be trained. Before leaving they had to be taught how to transfer Toney in and out of the car. They would gladly learn anything to have their boy home.

When the big moment arrived, Toney became apprehensive. He was very scared at the thought of riding in a car again. He began to feel better as he realized daddy, a professional driver for twenty-five years, would be behind the wheel.

The trip home seemed short. Getting out really felt good to Toney. He was enjoying the ride, but he couldn't wait to see Richmond.

When daddy's L.T.D. pulled off the interstate things started coming back to Toney. The Parham Road exit led to the very road where he had crashed. He had a sick feeling in his stomach. He tried to think of other things, but all he could think of was flashing lights and blood.

As the car rolled through Laurel, Toney saw the football field where he had been called "little Lineberry" so many times.

They crossed the railroad tracks he had put so many pennies on.

They passed the shopping center where he had joyfully wasted so many summer afternoons.

TWICE A CHAMPION

As the car headed for our house, all Toney could see were little kids running around playing. They seemed to be doing nothing, but in their minds they were probably fighting in World War II or driving in the Indianapolis 500.

"We're home!" Mama shouted as daddy pulled in that old familiar driveway. A tear rolled down Toney's face as he read the banner we had hung outside. "Welcome Home Toney!" Those were the three most wonderful words he could've read.

We all watched closely as daddy and C.B. got Toney out of the car. We knew it would be something we would all have to do many times.

The steps in front of our house were an omen of things to come. They just sat there, staring at the wheelchair, seemingly daring it to "come up me if you can." The inaccessible house was the only thing that didn't welcome Toney home with open arms.

We carried Toney up the stubborn steps and into the house where he had grown up.

As he entered, the memories hit him like a strong wind. The same T.V., the same sofa, the same piano. Toney looked at his fingers and thought how much he would miss them around here.

Toney seemed overwhelmed with all the people and all the celebration in the air. He appreciated it, but he wished it was just an ordinary Friday afternoon, with him kicked back on the sofa watching "Gunsmoke."

Donna rolled Toney back to his bedroom. When Toney saw that room it was as if all the terror and sadness in the world swarmed over him. Mama had left the room exactly the same. There were three shelves of trophies on the wall. His stereo was beside his bed. A big yellow surfboard was in a corner. His unicycle stood ready to be ridden in another corner. Beside his bed were the very boots he had been wearing in his crash.

He screamed and daddy came running back to the room. He arrived to find Toney crying on Donna's shoulder.

Would this horror ever end? Would Toney ever again be able to face life with a smile? This scene really hurt. It was supposed to be a happy occasion. If happy times meant sadness, what was left?

We all felt helpless as those two awful words floated through the house: "Why me?"

CHAPTER 6
ANOTHER HOSPITAL

*T*oney constantly fought the pain of seeing and feeling things that he once had. He constantly fought the hope that things would someday be like they once were. If he was to move on with his life, if he was to ever be happy again, he must learn to accept what had happened to him.

He constantly worked at this. He only wanted to think of the present and the future. He only wanted to think of positive things. This wasn't always possible, however. Each day he discovered something else that he could no longer do. Each day brought back another memory.

We all helped as much as possible. Mama rearranged his room. She got rid of his surfboard and his unicycle. New pictures were put on the walls. His trophies were packed away.

We never spoke of Toney's pre-accident life. The words wrestling or Mustang were never heard in our house. Instead of talking about things that might have been, we spoke of things that still might be.

As more weekends passed, as Toney came home more, he began to slowly accept his life there. He almost seemed happy there. At home, he wasn't just another patient. He was mama's only patient. He was special at home. He was not just another quad., lifting wrist weights and complaining about the food. At home, to us he was Toney, in a wheelchair now, who needed our help. At Towers he was Toney, in room 207, who was up to lifting one-and-a-half pounds.

Toney never spent another weekend at Towers. Every Friday someone would drive in front of the building to pick him up.

Nothing in the world mattered to him, as long as he could go home. He became obsessed with weekends.

Toney's pain continued at Towers. But the pain now wasn't like it used to be. Now it was a mental pain, the mental pain of wondering if he would ever get out of this awful place.

One day the old pain returned. A doctor, who looked like all the others, came in with a tray of instruments. Toney's heart fell to his stomach. Did he have pneumonia again? Is he not supposed to be breathing this well again? Are they going to amputate his legs? What's going on here? The doctor came at him with that tray of tools. He should have been wearing a sweat shirt with the word PAIN printed across the front of it.

"What's going on?" Toney whimpered.

"This is just routine procedure, Mr. Lineberry. I'm going to remove your trachea, the tube in your throat that the respirator was hooked up to, and replace it with this small button."

"Why?"

"Well, it's time for your throat to begin healing again. I'll replace the trachea with this small button, which can be reopened for emergency situations. Hold still for me please."

With a pliers-like instrument the doctor yanked the trachea from Toney's throat. Before the hole could close he inserted the button. Toney's throat throbbed with pain. It was like seventy-eight sore throats at one time.

The doctor thanked Toney for his cooperation and left the room. Just then daddy came clomping through the door with two chili dogs for Toney's lunch.

"Just the way you like 'em boy, lots of mustard."

With a voice that sounded like sandpaper would sound like if it could talk, Toney replied.

"I don't think I'm hungry."

Daddy ate the "dogs" and another chapter in Toney's book of pain was complete.

Toney got to know the inside of the Towers therapy room very well. He spent hours there. Not because he wanted to, but because there were so many people counting on him to get better.

Unfortunately, different people had different definitions of what getting better was. To the medical staff it meant a gradual strengthening of his biceps. To Toney it meant walking. He didn't care if his biceps got better. He just wanted to get out of the hospital and go home. And to Toney, a hospital is just what it was, it was not the promised land that would make him better.

Impatience collides with therapy. Toney's attitude was "I know I'm here for my own good, but I'm tired of lifting these stupid one-pound weights. Why can't I go home? Why do I have to stay here?"

The truth is, Toney had been there for three months and Towers really couldn't do much more for him. Mama and daddy spoke with the therapists about this while Toney was, they thought, asleep. It was decided he would be discharged. The news made the edges of Toney's mouth curl up as he kept his eyes closed.

"Have you thought about Woodrow Wilson? They have excellent facilities there. They can send him towards a career."

The edges of Toney's mouth tensed. He knew they were talking about another Godforsaken hospital.

"It's in Fishersville, another hour up 64."

"Oh God, it's farther" Toney thought as he struggled to keep his eyes closed and not start screaming.

Saying that Woodrow Wilson could help him more was all mama and daddy needed to hear. The papers would be put through for Toney to enter.

Toney pretended he hadn't overheard them talking about it when mama and daddy told him about the move.

"Please don't send me there! I do fine at home! It's just another hospital! Oh mama please! I just wanna go home!"

It was hard for mama and daddy to fight back the temptation of taking Toney home. Half of them wanted to make him feel better and half wanted to do what was best for him. As usual, the practical side won.

Toney felt better when he found out he would get to go home for three weeks before the move. He decided it was better than nothing and maybe mom and dad would see how well he got along and let him stay.

The day of departure arrived. Toney searched for something he would miss at Towers, but he couldn't find it. Paula gave him a big squeeze and he decided he would miss her. The second floor nurses waved as he got on the elevator. He decided he would miss them.

He rolled through the cafeteria on his way out. He decided he would definitely not miss that place. He asked daddy to stop for a minute and he watched as a therapist coached an obviously broken boy in a wheelchair. The boy flung his arms in desperation trying to stab a piece of food on his plate. The therapist put her arm around him as a tear rolled down the boy's cheek. Toney told daddy to go ahead. He shook his head and felt relieved to be getting out of this awful place where so many people were so sad.

To Toney, Towers was an awful place. But despite all the pain he felt there, both mental and physical, the hospital did a great deal for him. They transferred him from a very weak, gaunt-looking patient, fresh out of intensive care, to a stable quadriplegic with the use of and some strength in his arms. Toney was on his way to accepting his injury. Towers was a very big part of that.

Home! Home for three weeks! Toney loved that idea. As daddy and C.B. carried him up the steps of our house, he daydreamed about what he would do with himself for three weeks. His mind wandered for a moment. He thought about wrestling Danny again and maybe practicing football with the seniors at Laurel.

Thump!! Toney's chair backed into the T.V. as C.B. rolled him into the house. Reality set in. Toney looked at the T.V. and figured that's what he'd be doing for the next three weeks.

The next morning mama got Toney dressed. She was getting good at that. It's a lot harder putting clothes on someone else than it is putting them on yourself.

The sad thing is putting on Toney's clothes was the last thing mama had to do. First, his bowel program needed to be completed. It's not a wonderful thing to talk about, but people need to be aware. Toney cannot feel when he needs to go to the bathroom. This must be controlled, from bed, with suppositories. It's ugly and embarrassing, but somebody must do it, and mama did.

It gets even worse. Sometimes these artificial means don't take care of it and bowel accidents occur in public. I can't think of anything more embarrassing.

After that, mama puts on Toney's leg bag. This is a device that allows him to urinate through a tube strapped to his leg. This tube or bag can burst. Embarrassment is always just a malfunction away.

The three weeks at home seemed like forever to Toney. Being at home was somehow not as great anymore. He did something he had never done in his life. He just sat around. He would've twiddled his thumbs if he could've moved them.

The old house was the same. He would just sit in it remembering old times, remembering he and his girlfriend on the couch or slamming me on top of the rubber plant. He found himself wishing he wasn't there. An awful thought came to his mind: he didn't want to be anywhere. He shook that thought out of his mind and decided home was his best option.

Sometimes he would sit outside. The old neighborhood looked the same, but not to Toney. He couldn't climb the oak tree in our front yard. He couldn't pull his car in the yard and wash it. He couldn't ride his bike to the store for a cold Mountain Dew.

Sitting out on that sidewalk Toney felt almost like an elderly person. The neighbors would stop and talk with him. He appreciated it, but he often thought they were just pitying him.

He would sit and think. Oh how he longed to get up in freezing weather and deliver newspapers with dogs chasing him. Oh how he longed to not be able to eat for six days, so he could make his weight and twist a kid into a pretzel on the wrestling mat. Oh how he longed for a concussion at Laurel Little League. He sat there longing for pain. "None of that stuff really hurt," he thought.

An acorn clunked his head. He swatted his arm in disgust and went sprawling out of his chair. He screamed. This had never happened before. "I can't even sit in a stupid wheelchair!"

Help quickly arrived and everything was all right. New thoughts popped into Toney's mind, however. He was realizing that he didn't have any balance. He had been told this, but had never experienced it. He wondered when he would ever learn how to be handicapped. He decided he didn't want to learn.

Toney was determined that he would be normal. He really wanted to go out on the town again with his friends. They gladly helped all they could, but things didn't always work out. There was many a night out with the gang when Toney would have one of those embarrassing situations mentioned earlier. His friends, good fellows like Danny Kelley, John Reid, and Robert Goodman, would understand. It didn't help much. They would just take Toney home and he would lay in bed trying not to think about the night. He wondered if anything good would ever happen to him again. He wouldn't admit it, but he would feel sorry for himself.

Much to Toney's dismay, the three weeks came to an end. He sat in the living room with me and Terry as mama packed the last of his things. We tried to talk to him, but he seemed preoccupied. He looked so sad.

Toney sat there feeling awful that he had let these three weeks slip by. He felt like he had wasted the time feeling sorry for himself. He wished he had been a little more cheerful towards his family. He promised himself if he ever came home again for an extended period of time things would be different.

Mama let me stay home from school that day and Terry took a day of vacation so we could ride with daddy to take Toney to Woodrow Wilson. Toney sat in the front seat and Terry and I sat in back. It was obvious we were all trying to talk about happy things and not think about our destination.

I mentioned my wrestling team and Toney pretended to be interested. He asked me how I was doing. I didn't have the nerve to tell him I had quit. I was ashamed of myself. I thought he would wonder why I wasn't more like him. I sat there wishing I could tell him that the only reason I started was him, and now other things seemed more important.

It's pretty much a straight shot up I-64 to Woodrow Wilson

Rehabilitation Center. This day, however, Terry asked daddy to ride through the town of Waynesboro on the way. She said she just liked riding through town, but we all knew she was just trying to prolong the trip.

Waynesboro is a nice town. It's kind of hilly and is full of fast-food restaurants. It's very close to Woodrow Wilson and would end up being a town Toney saw a lot.

Daddy pulled his L.T.D. onto the long blacktop driveway of Woodrow Wilson. It was a hot and sticky day and the sun shined on the sign at the entrance as Toney read it. "Welcome to Woodrow Wilson Rehabilitation Center." Rehabilitation, that one word came rushing at Toney and made him shake his head. "When will I ever stop rehabilitating?" he thought.

Toney's rehabilitation really was helping him. He had improved enough to come to this place, which was really much less like a hospital. Their emphasis was on the future, and the people there were called students, not patients. Toney had been told all this but he had grown not to trust any place away from home that was associated with his handicap.

When we pulled up, the place did look different. Patients were sitting outside and it appeared to have a college atmosphere. Therapists were waiting for us and they took Toney and daddy into a room for a meeting. Terry and I waited in the cafeteria.

"Welcome Toney." Toney forced a small smile that pulsated with skepticism.

"The purpose of this meeting is for you to set goals for yourself that we hope to help you achieve."

Goals? What did that mean? Toney wasn't yet convinced that he would never walk again. Why should he set goals? The therapists and counselors were determined to get goals from him and they finally did.

"Well, if I can't walk, I want to at least be independent. I've seen people in wheelchairs driving. I'd like to be able to do that someday."

A hush came over the room. Lots of "wells" and "uhs" were murmured. In a discouraging tone the questioners told Toney that no one with his level of injury had ever driven.

They continued with lots of medical jargon but Toney didn't hear them. All he heard was them saying he would never be able to drive. He wondered when people would stop discouraging him. Never in his life had he been in such a negative position.

Toney couldn't believe they said he would never drive. "How will I get around? I'm gonna have to sit in that front yard for the rest of my life."

The meeting left Toney very discouraged. He felt down and out, like he had no future at all. He didn't care about rehabilitating. He just wanted to be happy again.

Me, Terry, daddy, and Toney, went to his room for the "checking in." It was not like checking into a hotel. This was not a vacation. Smiles were rare.

Toney's room was very big. It had a college dorm look and held three roommates. There was a bathroom as you walked in, with a gigantic shower. The spacious room had two beds and a T.V. on each side. We entered and rolled Toney to his bed. His three roommates watched as a terrible, typical, scene crept upon us. We left and he had to stay.

Toney had only been in his room ten minutes when he developed his opinion of it. He hated it. It depressed him and he wished he had the strength to catch daddy's car and hop in. He sat by his bed and looked over at his roommates. One was lying in bed propped to his side. He explained to Toney that he had pressure sores on his rear end and he couldn't sit in a wheelchair. "You'll get 'em soon, everybody does. Boy, you're gonna hate it here!"

Toney fought back a tear as he looked towards another roommate. This one was a bit more pleasant. Toney recognized him as an old friend from Towers. He knew the ropes at Woodrow and would eventually show Toney around.

The final roommate was sitting in his wheelchair, towards the window, with his back turned away from Toney. After a few minutes the chair buzzed around towards Toney. The boy sat there completely still. He had been paralyzed from the neck down in a diving accident. He had a straw in his mouth connected to a box that controlled an electric wheelchair. He looked at Toney with sad eyes and tilted his head down, forcing the mechanical chair out the door.

This guy scared the hell out of Toney. He didn't know if he would end up in his shape or not.

That night was one of the worst of Toney's life. He lay there, with three broken bodies sleeping around him. He stared at the ceiling and wondered if he would spend the rest of his life bouncing from hospital to hospital, meeting new handicapped people and fighting sadness every day.

Life at Woodrow Wilson wasn't that much different than at Towers. The only difference was more "advanced" rehabilitation and stronger patients. Woodrow was bigger and had more things to do. It offered more and tried to push the handicapped towards a normal life. It was regarded as one of the finest rehabilitation centers on the East Coast. It was the last stop for patients, where they could learn to adjust to the handicapped world. Toney didn't want to adjust, he just wanted to go home.

One word was said over and over. Therapy, therapy, therapy. It was what life was. "You have to make yourself stronger! You'll never make it weak!" The therapists (there's that word again) would preach constantly.

The therapy began to show signs of perhaps working. Toney began to feel stronger and he felt the therapy coming easier and easier. All those mornings on the mat lifting small wrist weights were beginning to pay off. Much to his surprise, he began to gradually be able to push his wheelchair. It was a struggle, but with a little hard work he could push himself from place to place.

Every morning after physical therapy the students were required, if able, to push themselves to lunch. It was a long journey to the cafeteria, and required going outside down a long sidewalk. Toney made that journey day after day, each day his arms would throb with pain. This pain, however, felt good to him. It was the pain of pushing yourself. It was the way he used to feel after running ten miles. He liked the thought of "working out" again.

Toney was human. Some days he didn't feel like making that long push. He didn't care about working out. On these days, he would get a push if possible. Along with handicapped patients, Woodrow Wilson also has a separate facility for emotionally disturbed patients. These patients would share the same cafeteria with the handicapped patients. One day, Toney asked a boy if he would mind giving him a push to the cafeteria. The boy was very nice.

"Well, sure!"

The boy pushed Toney's chair and for the first few yards Toney kept thanking him. Sort of like a freight train, the boy kept picking up more and more speed. Suddenly the "thank you's" turned to "hey what are you doing!" The speed got faster, the boy was at a sprint. Buildings were zooming by Toney and he began to scream. It was as if the boy forgot Toney was in the chair and he thought he had a toy! Finally, in one, big, triumphant push the boy heaved Toney into a row of bushes.

The bushes seemed to swallow Toney. Leaves were in his ear, branches were in his hair. His body was tangled into all sorts of positions. He began screaming and no one came. Finally, after thirty minutes, a very angry and a very hungry Toney was helped into his chair by a male nurse.

While sitting in an empty cafeteria, munching on a Clark bar, Toney decided that he had been taught a lesson. From then on, he would push himself.

Afternoons meant occupational therapy. Toney tried to dress himself, but that came very difficult. It wasn't known if he would ever be able to do that. He hoped he would never be so alone that he would have to dress himself.

The hardest thing Toney had to relearn in O.T. was to write again. In order to write, he had to be able to wrap his fingers around a pen and to be able to move his wrist. Toney could do neither. He was forced to prop the pen between his limp, "dead," fingers. Instead of moving his wrist he would move his entire arm. Coordination is much more difficult and neatness is rare. Toney spent hours just making circling motions on paper trying to build coordination. He practiced writing his name thousands of times. He was tired of writing "X" when he signed something.

Occupational therapy continually stressed that being handicapped was not the end of the world. They promised career opportunities and a chance for a normal life. To Toney, these were only dreams. It was like a poor man hoping to be rich someday.

Nights were often very rough times for Toney. He spent many hours in the rec-room playing cards or backgammon or reading. The darkness often watered his eyes and put a lump in his throat. He missed just sitting on the sofa watching T.V. with his girlfriend or family. He longed to be out with his friends.

Some nights Toney was fortunate enough to be able to go to Waynesboro with some of his new friends. One was able to drive and that made for some exciting times.

One night Toney and two of his roommates piled into the boy's van and headed for Waynesboro, whooping and hollering. They wheeled into a pizza restaurant and they all began screaming obscenities at a man who had parked in a handicapped parking space. This may not seem like a big deal, but to people in wheelchairs those spaces mean a lot. Quite often, those spaces determine whether a driver can get his wheelchair lift out or not.

The driver was the angriest of the group. As the others laughed, he pulled his van up beside the fellow's car. He swung his lift out, and began slamming it on and off the hood of the car.

"Let's see if I can get my lift out here!"

Slam! Crunch! Crash!

"Yeh, I think you've got it!" one passenger yelled.

Slam! Crunch! Crash!

"Sure it'll fit, try it again!" another passenger added.

Slam! Crunch! Crash!

Finally the surprised fellow came running out of the restaurant. "What the hell are you doing!?"

In a sarcastic tone, the angry driver said "Oh, is this your car? We just wanted to get out and go get some pizza but something was blocking my lift."

If you ever park in a handicapped parking space, even if you're just running inside to pick up a pizza, don't be surprised if you return to a dented hood.

Every other night was shower night in Toney's room. The bathroom contained a big roll-in shower with four stalls. The patients would transfer into what is called a shower chair. This is simply a wheelchair that is sat in while showering. The patients are then sort of herded into the room. The attendants scrub them down and they're rolled out almost like in a car wash. These were embarrassing times for Toney. It wasn't like being in the locker room with his teammates, showering down after a tough workout. It was more like a shy, broken person being washed by a total stranger.

Toney would lay awake every night and dream of Friday when he could go home. He never spent one weekend at Woodrow Wilson. Everyone knew how important it was for him to go home. Going home on weekends made his life continue somehow. To him, the week at Woodrow sort of left his life still. At home it moved on a little.

Some of Toney's friends really stuck by him during these times. Danny was always there. He had always looked up to Toney, and he still did. To him, Toney was no different now, he just couldn't walk. He was determined that a wheelchair would not stand in the way of their friendship.

Toney was miserable during the week. We visited as often as we could. Mama still visited regularly. Daddy spent many an hour watching him lift those wrist weights.

One night, Donna, Mike and I decided to visit Toney. As we pulled into the parking lot we expected the usual rec-room atmosphere to be there. Much to our surprise, the room was filled with music and women dancing. We quietly slipped in to see belly dancers dancing in a circle formed by the wheelchairs. Some of the patients were yelling and really having a good time. Toney just sat there with a puzzled look on his face. Mike and I died laughing when one of the dancers draped a piece of clothing over Toney's head. He fought to get it off but you could see a smile as the girl gave him a kiss. He later admitted that it felt good.

Woodrow Wilson was not just a place for rehabilitation. They tried to instill an attitude in their students. All handicapped citizens, they reasoned, need an attitude of self-esteem. Woodrow tried to make them feel that they were an important part of society.

This attitude was encouraged during counseling sessions. Toney's counselor was a fellow named Walt Wilson. Walt taught Toney how to deal with his handicap. He made Toney feel like maybe there is a future. He would tell him stories of handicapped people who really made it big. Toney began to dream. Walt told him that hard work was the key. Toney thought he had been working hard. What would he have to do? He wondered and dreamed. He decided that if he could just get out of the hospital there would be no stopping him.

Toney was very determined that he would drive someday. He would sit and remember himself tooling around in his Mustang. He longed to be able to get behind the wheel again. He thought that would give him the independence he needed to go on with his life. He talked about driving all of the time. We all knew that if there was any way possible he would drive again someday.

Much time was spent doing nothing at Woodrow Wilson. Toney and others would sit in their wheelchairs out on a patio and just think. To pass the time they would often talk. Sometimes they would talk about the food of the day, sometimes about their life at home, sometimes about things that meant nothing at all. Sometimes the talks would have meaning and even teach a lesson.

One afternoon Toney and two of his roommates were on the patio talking. It was a Monday and they were all in particularly grumpy moods.

The scene from the patio was very pleasant. There was a beautiful view of the Blue Ridge Mountains.

The mood of the young men was definitely not pleasant. One of them, a paraplegic paralyzed from the waist down, started the conversation on this afternoon.

"Man, I hate it here! If I could only walk I'd be out of here. I wouldn't need no ride, I'd just walk home."

Toney couldn't believe that the boy had the nerve to complain.

"You don't have any problems! You can move your hands! You dress yourself, you spin around here doing wheelies. Man, you've got it made! If I could just move my hands I'd push myself back to Richmond. I wouldn't need no luggage or nothing. I'd be outta here!"

Toney's other roommate, a quadriplegic paralyzed from the neck down, just sat there staring at them with a look of disgust on his face. He rarely spoke, but did on this day.

"You've both got a lot of nerve! If I could just move my arms to brush my teeth I'd be happy."

He tilted the straw in his mouth down and his chair buzzed off. The other boy slowly pushed himself behind him.

Toney sat there, alone, with a tear rolling down his cheek. That conversation really hit him hard. Maybe he didn't have it so bad. It could actually be worse. He shook his head and thought how terrible that would be. He decided that he may not be able to move his hands, but he was gonna make the most of his arms. He would never again look at his handicap quite the same.

CHAPTER 7
THE DREAM

*T*oney counted the days until weekends came. He wouldn't be at Woodrow Wilson much longer, but he still refused to stay there on weekends. Every Friday afternoon he would sit out on the patio, a suitcase or two by his side, and wait for daddy's white L.T.D. to pull up.

One Friday was especially memorable for Toney and daddy. The sun seemed to be waving goodbye as it slowly ducked behind a mountain. Toney asked daddy to pull over to a scenic view area. He desperately wanted to take in this peaceful, happy sight, one that he rarely saw at Woodrow Wilson. For what seemed like hours they sat there, the two of them, and watched that ball of red slowly disappear.

"Daddy, it's gonna take a lot more than a broken neck to get us down, isn't it?"

"You better believe it, son."

A tear formed in daddy's eye as he pulled on to the interstate. He felt better than he ever had about the accident. He knew he had a fighter on his hands.

A big question in everyone's mind was how Toney would make it in that little house in Laurel Park? How would he climb those steps and make it around those narrow halls?

As time went on mama and daddy decided that he wouldn't have to just "make it." They decided to move away from their home of twenty years and build a new, handicap-accessible home. It would mean that they would move away from their friends and further from work. But worst of all, it would mean that they would now have house payments of over $400.00, instead of their usual $72.00 a month. They never complained.

They knew Toney couldn't live in our old house, so they began to search for a place to build a new one. They found that place in Goochland County, between Richmond and Charlottesville.

One Friday daddy got off the interstate in Goochland to show Toney where his new home would be. They rode down lots of old, country roads. Houses were few and cows were plenty. As daddy weaved around curve after curve Toney decided he must be in the middle of nowhere.

While sitting in the driveway of the lot, daddy promised to fix the house up just for Toney. Toney smiled but deep down he was hurting. He hated the idea of moving to this country place, so far from his friends. He wondered how he would get back and forth to school. He decided he wouldn't say anything to mom and dad. He thought they had been through enough.

It's ironic that this new house was supposed to be so good for Toney, yet it made everyone so sad. I suppose I was the worst about it. I thought moving away was absolutely horrible. I would have to go to a new school and make new friends. I felt like I was going to have to start a new life and I was angry. As if I had been injured, I began asking "why me?" I remember sitting in my room in Laurel Park packing my things, crying, and wondering how everything that was so good could be so bad.

Toney spent hours thinking and wondering. What would he be doing now if he hadn't hit that sheet of ice? Wrestling practice was drawing near, he knew he would be gearing up for that, probably preparing to defend his championship. He saw marriage, kids, a little house, and a white picket fence. He used to look forward to the passing time. Now it just meant something else bad could happen. He decided it wasn't fair and he grimaced at the thought of more time passing.

Time did bring some good things, however. It took him out of hospitals. It made him stronger. It let what had happened slowly sink in. Time would eventually tell Toney that moping and feeling sorry for yourself accomplishes nothing.

Coach Donahue's "Toney Lineberry Fund" was beginning to pay off. Support had poured in from everyone Toney knew and from many he didn't know. Over $16,000 was raised and it waited in an account for Toney.

Even though hospital officials had said Toney would never be able to drive, it was decided that some of the money would be used to buy a van. Even if he could never drive it, it would make for much easier transportation when people had to drive him places.

That fund was truly a blessing. Toney got his dream: a blue van. As he sat in it he decided there was some good in the world. He felt like everyone who had contributed was part owner of the van. He hoped he wouldn't let them down. He would give anything if he could drive it.

Toney's days at Woodrow Wilson were getting to their later stages. It was like he was a senior in high school. He got tired of people asking him what he was going to do when he got out of the hospital. He desperately wanted to answer them but he couldn't. Everyone was only concerned about him, but he wished they would just leave him alone.

Where would Toney's life take him next? He had dreamed of getting out of the hospital for months. Now the day was near and he wasn't excited at all. He had a very big decision to make. Should he try to go back to high school and get his diploma? Or should he take the easy way out and stay at home, get tutored, and get his G.E.D.?

He really wanted to go back to school with his friends, but he wondered if his friends would be able to handle it when he came rolling towards them. He was once strong and independent, a ladies man, who had many friends. He was once a champion. Now he would be a crippled senior needing someone to carry his books for him.

He wondered if going back was worth it. The only thing he ever liked about school was wrestling. Now all he would be able to do is watch. The decision was his, his alone. Everyone would understand if he took the easy way out. He didn't. He decided he was going to fight.

"Enroll me back in Hermitage. My life is not gonna stop here!"

Toney's last day at Woodrow Wilson was a very big one. He was filled with joy and relief. He beamed a huge smile when he saw mama and daddy pull up in his van.

He said goodbye to his friends there. He wished them luck and said he would miss them, but he couldn't wait to get home and renew his old friendships.

Two big boards formed a ramp to get Toney into his new van. It was a tough push for someone to get him up, but it was easier than lifting him into a seat. He would ride there in the van, never thinking about a safety belt. Little did he know that he was in a very dangerous situation should the van crash.

Toney could care less about safety as daddy drove the van down the long Woodrow Wilson driveway. He had a little grin on his face, a grin of victory. He felt like he had survived a sentence in hell. He decided it was over now and that he would now go and live his life.

Woodrow Wilson deserves a lot of credit. They made Toney realize that this was the way it was going to be. I suppose you could even say that he accepted what had happened to him. Woodrow made him the best possible paralyzed eighteen-year-old he could be.

Things were getting better, but huge doses of anxiety quickly set in. Toney wasn't home for long when he began to get scared about the return to school. For the first time he realized that he wouldn't be the same at school. He had awful nightmares of no one recognizing him or of being stranded in a hall, unable to push himself.

All Toney wanted was to be normal at school. He remembered seeing kids in wheelchairs when he was in school. He remembered feeling sorry for them but not really knowing what to say to them. He wished he would've just treated them like people.

There was no question that Toney was a different person. Most of the things he relied on before his accident were no longer there. He no longer had his strength, his stamina, or even his self-control. He now depended on someone else for almost everything. He didn't have that cocky "I'm gonna tackle the world" attitude anymore. Now he just did what he could and hoped everyone would understand how he is now.

Friends. What would anyone do without them? To Toney, they were everything. They were a symbol that he was still a normal person. They made him realize that he was still special. It was easy for us, his family, to accept him now, but for friends it was very awkward. Those who could accept him—and many could not—meant more to Toney than anything.

One of these friends went beyond just accepting Toney. His name is Robert Goodman, a former wrestling teammate. He cared about how Toney would get to school. He offered to drive him back and forth everyday. This was no easy task, since Hermitage was about fifteen miles, one way, from our new home. Robert represents the definition of unselfish. He was determined that Toney would make a smooth transition back into high school.

To say that Toney was nervous about his first day back to school would be an understatement. He was terrified. He slept none the night before, just staring at the ceiling thinking, hoping and praying. He thought about how easy things used to be and how hard this would be. He hoped he could just fit right back in. He hoped that he wouldn't fall on his face, that he wouldn't seem "deformed" to everybody.

The big morning came. Robert got there early, just like he said he would. We all seemed a bit nervous as daddy and Robert put Toney in the car. That fifteen mile trip seemed like a hundred miles to Toney that morning. He hated the thought of Robert having to make this journey twice a day. "I hope this is worth it," he thought.

Hermitage hadn't changed at all. The parking lots, the stadium, the brick buildings were all the same. Toney's heart was beating a mile a minute as Robert pulled into the handicapped parking space. The school was the same, but Toney felt different. He didn't just pull up in his Mustang, jump out and run in. Getting out of the car and going in was now a task.

As Robert rolled him through the big double doors at Hermitage, Toney saw two people that brought back some bitter memories. Cuddled against a radiator were his ex-girlfriend and the ex-friend who had promised to "take care of her."

Toney had long since gotten over the girl. He had realized that he now had more important things to worry about. Nevertheless, he would never forget what his friend had said to him. "I guess he took care of her," Toney thought.

Many people flocked around Toney's chair as he rolled down the hall. Some girls hugged him and some guys slugged him. These were the people who would be there the rest of the way. These were the people who realized that Toney hadn't changed, that he was just in a wheelchair.

Many people couldn't handle seeing Toney the way he was. Some people who Toney had been great friends with, people whom he had grown up with, would walk by and turn their heads real quick. Toney would begin to say something to them, but the hurt of it all would overcome him and he'd let them pass. He didn't lack friends by any means, but he'll never understand why he lost so many friends just because he was paralyzed. I can't help but think that perhaps these people had more of a problem than Toney did. If one loses friends every time they change, they will be very lonely before they die.

Toney joked around a lot at school. He tried desperately to prove that he was the same old Toney. He really wanted people to be comfortable around him.

As time passed things got better and better. A routine developed, and Toney slowly began to feel part of it all again. Robert began driving Toney's van back and forth, and before long that van turned into a school bus. Each morning and afternoon the van would become loaded down with Hermitage Panthers. Most of the time they would go to school but sometimes they would head for the river or another typical high school partying place. Toney was very happy with his friends. For the first time since the accident he was a part of everything again. In some small way he was normal again. Sometimes, on those trips, he felt he was the old Toney again.

But he was not the old Toney. Accepting this would be a long, drawn out process for both he and his friends and family. There were many obstacles in his life now. There would be a lot of pain mixed in with overcoming them.

School came hard to Toney. Someone would have to write for him. He stuck out in the classrooms. He couldn't just sit at a desk and he was always in the way. The teachers were very good to him, sometimes too good. By being so nice some of them made him feel abnormal.

Often Toney's obstacles would be mental. He had been used to some sort of physical activity his entire life. When he would see an athletic team practicing, it would rip him apart inside. The thought of never being able to wrestle again hurt so bad. He tried one afternoon to watch the team practice. As his friends rolled around the mat in the wrestling room, struggling and straining, his eyes began to water. He tried frantically to fight back the tears, but he couldn't. He sat there and wept as the team stopped and looked at him. Coach Donahue consoled him. It was the weakest he had ever been in that room.

Some days at school were absolutely horrible. Malfunctions with the bowel and bladder are inevitable with the paralyzed person. When this happened at school it was the worst thing Toney thought could ever happen to him. Imagine having to go home from school because you urinated in your pants.

The school year can bring many exciting, eventful, memorable things to students. From dances to football games, kids have the chance to enjoy all that school has to offer. All his life Toney had been right in the middle of these activities. Now it wasn't easy to be involved. Luckily, he had many great people with him who were determined that he would have the chance to do everything.

Toney may have been weakened by his injury, but his attraction to women was not diminished in the least. He slowly began to be able to talk to them again. He not only began to talk to them, he began to ask them out. It was a great feeling for him to be with girls again. His ex-girlfriend's departure hurt him very badly, and he used to wonder if he'd ever be with a girl again. This is not something he should've worried about. Girls were still very attracted to him.

Toney's dates were not like they used to be. He was forced to always double date so he would have a driver and someone to lift him in and out of the van. He kept a big "living room" chair in the van for the girls to sit in. The dates couldn't involve a lot of getting in and out of the van: it was too much trouble. Drive-in movies and restaurants were common. They often just rode around or sat in the van at a romantic spot.

It was established before hand on Toney's dates that whoever was driving him would take his date home first, and then get out of the van while Toney said goodbye to his date. One night it was especially cold and Robert was the driver. He got out so Toney could say goodbye not knowing that he would end up freezing his butt off. It took Toney an especially long time to say his goodbyes to this girl. After awhile, Toney glanced in the mirror and saw Robert huddled next to the exhaust pipe trying to keep warm. Toney chuckled and told the girl she better go before Robert gets frostbite.

As the school year went on Toney began to wonder what the future held for him. While sitting in that wheelchair, he couldn't see himself leading a productive life. He was scared to death at the thought of sitting or lying around for the rest of his life, waiting to die. He searched desperately within his mind for a goal, for something to shoot for. He planned to graduate in June, but then what? These thoughts stayed with him and bothered him constantly.

Toney encountered many problems that others never think of. A big problem is the lack of circulation. His paralyzed body has weak blood circulation. This causes parts of the body to become either very hot or very cold. In the summer, on hot days, his body can't perspire the normal amount, causing constant overheating. In the winter the lack of circulation causes him to be miserably cold. Imagine having to plan your life to make sure you are always near an air conditioner or heater. Toney went home from school many a day because he was either so cold even jackets couldn't keep him warm or because he was so overheated only cold washcloths on his body could keep him cool.

Balance was another problem. One should never take it for granted. Toney has very little. Sitting in a chair can be difficult. Reaching to pick something up can be difficult. Sometimes, even lying in bed can be a task.

Beds can often be a terrible menace. Toney can't feel his lower body when lying in bed. You may not notice it, but you're constantly shifting in bed to keep the pressure off of your behind. Toney can't feel the sensation that makes you shift, and awful bedsores often develop. These bedsores are serious welps, and can sometimes be deadly. Many patients become bedridden or even hospitalized because of these sores that occurred because they were positioned in bed or in their wheelchair the wrong way. Someone must get up twice a night to turn Toney's paralyzed body.

Toney loved his van. He would spend hours just looking at it or watching someone wash it. He would give anything if he could drive it. The people at Woodrow Wilson had told him he couldn't drive, but he couldn't help dreaming that someday, somehow he would get a little better or something would happen that would allow him to drive. He had taken test after test at Woodrow that indicated he couldn't drive. But he still, somewhere in the back of his mind, stored some hope that he would again be behind the wheel.

One afternoon Toney was reading a magazine called *Paraplegic News*. He didn't care that much for reading, but there wasn't much else to do. He didn't particularly want to read this magazine, but he was on their mailing list and it was all that was lying around. As he flipped through the pages he noticed an ad that caught his eye. "We Teach High Level Quadriplegics To Drive." He didn't understand. He had been told that only low level quadriplegics could drive. He figured it was an advertising gimmick, but he called the number just to see what they had to say.

"I read your ad. I'm not sure I believe it!"

"We have a new technology called 'zero effort.' It allows some highly injured people to use hand controls and steer easily through hydraulics."

Toney didn't really understand everything the man said, but he understood enough to know that there may be a chance for him to drive. The man on the phone told Toney to come down to North Carolina and they would evaluate his ability to drive.

Toney was very hesitant to ask mama and daddy about this new found chance to drive. After all, he had already torn up one car and almost killed himself. Why should they want him to drive again?

When Toney finally did pop the question they were skeptical about it, thinking it was just a magazine ad. But after making a few calls about it, they decided they wanted Toney to have the chance.

Mama was very excited for Toney, but she was very scared that he would be disappointed. She wasn't sure that he could handle another setback. Daddy felt the same way, but they knew how much he wanted to try. They made the arrangements for the trip to North Carolina.

Robert and Toney took the van, followed by me, mama, and daddy. It was the biggest trip of Toney's life. He was scheduled to be tested on a simulator to see if he could handle the new equipment. When all the tests were completed a very important verdict would be reached: The instructor would either say "you can drive" or "I'm sorry, your injury is too severe."

The tests took a day and a half and we all began to grow restless. I must have bugged mama for a quarter for the candy machine a hundred times.

When it was all over Toney wasn't sure how he'd done. He sat in the waiting room with us and he didn't have a very confident look on his face. He was anticipating the worst. So many terrible things had happened to him lately, he grew not to expect good things to happen.

Toney's instructor came to the waiting room with a clipboard full of papers. No emotion showed on his face. There is no way that he could've possibly known the importance of the announcement he was about to make. I prayed that it was good news. I was tired of seeing Toney hurt.

The instructor's cigar smoke filled the room. "It looks like you can handle our equipment. It'll take a lot of training, but you can handle it." The instructor seemed puzzled as we all yelled for joy and hugged Toney. Toney smiled like I had never seen him smile before. His dream was going to become a reality. It would mean more independence than he thought he would ever have.

It seems that in front of every silver lining there is a cloud. The equipment that would allow Toney to drive cost more than $10,000. The Toney Lineberry fund had run out and the money had to come from somewhere. Daddy had just built a new house and finding the money would be difficult. He decided that he would get it somehow, and the van was left in North Carolina for the installation of the equipment.

Toney was as excited as a pigeon in the park about the controls being put on his van. You would've thought he was getting some sort of life or death organ transplant. I suppose to him it was that important. Being able to drive was the difference between sitting at home most of the time, just hoping for a ride somewhere, and getting out in the world, perhaps even making something of his life. It would be three months before the van was ready. Toney bounced off the walls in anticipation.

Slowly but surely Toney was beginning to get back to doing something he had always done a great deal of. It was something that most high school kids do and something he missed a lot. Party!! He got back in to partying, but in a different way. Through dealing with his injury, he learned that it is necessary to stay in control. He knew in the back of his mind that if it wasn't for a party he would be walking today.

Nevertheless, when the situation called for it, Toney began going to parties again. It seemed like every time he went out, there were five or ten people with him. Toney felt comfortable around people, and people were feeling comfortable around him. People were finally beginning to be able to see past his wheelchair.

Toney very seldom actually went in to a party. He would sit in his van, or whatever he was riding in, and part of the party would come to him. Just like the kitchen or living room in some parties, his vehicle became a central part of the party.

School was a pain for Toney. He had more desire to finish than he did to learn. He enjoyed his friends and the fun that goes along with school, but he hated having to learn. He wasn't dumb by any means, but other things were just more important to him. Before his accident those things were his car and athletics. Now those things were learning little things again, learning to function again. He was too busy learning to put his pants on to learn algebra. He just wanted to finish school, forget it, and go on with his life. I suppose the old saying "the grass is always greener on the other side" applied here. Toney had the idea that if he could just finish high school and learn to drive, everything would be alright.

The weather constantly picked at Toney. Winter was the worst. He would go to school freezing every day. He couldn't understand it, he had never been cold before. He would bundle up for all he was worth every morning, but still freeze on the way to school. He began to long for spring, and he hoped the next winter would be better.

When warm weather did arrive there were mixed emotions. Toney was very happy not to be cold anymore, but oh how he longed for those warm weather activities he had spent his life doing. He would ride by a pond and wish he could dive in. He would ride by a baseball diamond and wish he could play. He would see a kid riding his bike down the street and he would yearn to be ten again. He saw all these things and thought how he used to take everything for granted. He wished he would've slowed down and enjoyed those younger days more. He wished he would've realized that he wouldn't always be able to do those things. One of the saddest things about Toney's injury was that he had to grow up too fast.

Toney dated very often. I remember me and my dad getting a kick out of all the girls he went out with. "That's my boy," daddy would say.

Winter meant Winter Carnival, a very popular Hermitage tradition. This is a dance where everyone takes a date and dances the night away. One couple from the senior class is chosen king and queen of Winter Carnival.

As mama dressed Toney in his Winter Carnival tux, he thought back to previous dances. He remembered being decked out. He would strut on to the floor, his girl on his arm, grinning from ear to ear.

There would be no strutting on this night. Instead, Toney's date would push him and he would struggle not to fall out of his wheelchair onto the combination basketball court–dance floor.

Robert, Danny, and John picked Toney up at our house. Mama took pictures and straightened Toney's bow tie as they went out the door.

On the way to pick up his date, Toney was nervous. But he was determined to make sure his date had a good time. He was determined to be normal.

The group of seven strolled into the dance, pushing Toney. The other six hit the dance floor. Toney's date felt awkward. She didn't care that much about dancing, but she was afraid Toney felt bad because he couldn't dance with her. Toney sensed this. "Roll me out there! Let's dance!" A crowd applauded as she swung his arm to the "Bee Gees."

At the end of the night something happened that no one expected. Toney and his date were voted king and queen of Winter Carnival. As his wheelchair swayed back and forth during the king and queen's solo dance, Toney felt truly like a king. He knew he had lots of friends in that gymnasium.

It wasn't until he got home that he had an awful thought: Was it pity or popularity? He carried these mixed emotions for a long time. Things like this were just another step towards accepting what had happened to him. It's terrible that good things sometimes made him hurt inside.

Toney counted the days before his van would be ready. He couldn't wait to get behind the wheel again, to be in control. Daddy called about the van every week but it seemed like every week the man said "one more week, Mr. Lineberry."

When the day did come Toney was so excited you would've

thought he just got out of a hospital. The van looked completely different. It had a big control box on the outside with switches to open the electric door and to swing his wheelchair lift out and down.

The driver's seat had been taken out so the wheelchair could roll under the steering wheel. There were special controls and buttons everywhere. It looked like the cockpit of an airplane.

Toney would get in and just sit behind the steering wheel, dreaming of the day he could drive it. It would take a lot of training and practice before that dream could be realized.

The training was not such a drawn out process. The man in North Carolina just showed Toney how to work everything, and sent him on his way.

Practicing was quite a different story. Toney spent as much time as he could at the church parking lot trying to get used to driving. He would putt along at three miles-per-hour, stopping and starting, turning and backing. He was determined to teach himself how to drive this van.

Our sister, Cathy, spent hours riding with Toney while he practiced. He moved up to a larger parking lot and began to go faster. He slowly gained confidence behind the wheel and eventually mastered the "parking lot scene."

The van still had a seat you could bolt under the steering wheel and the foot pedals were still there. It was tricky to drive, however, because the steering and brakes were super sensitive. They were four times more sensitive than the normal power brakes and steering. It was specially designed for Toney's strength and it was tough for anyone else to drive. Robert got good at driving it, however, as he drove he and Toney to school each day.

Toney's senior year was coming to a close. He was going to make it. He had survived all those times when he wasn't sure if his wheelchair was going to allow him to do it. He began to see light at the end of the tunnel. Maybe the handicapped Toney could accomplish something.

Toney practiced driving his van religiously. As he cruised through parking lots he gained confidence. He had a wonderful feeling that he was ready to drive on the road. He decided he wanted to try it on the last day of school.

Toney asked mama and daddy if he could drive his final day and they seemed shocked. But they knew how hard he had practiced and they reluctantly agreed he should give it a try.

Toney's heart was rapidly beating as Robert buckled him under the steering wheel. Everything seemed to be going in slow motion as the power lock down system locked his chair into place. He took a deep breath as he placed his paralyzed hand over the "quad knob," a knob atttached to the wheel that would allow him to steer. He backed out of the driveway. His dream of driving again was coming true.

Things were going smoothly as Toney tooled down the highway in his shiny blue van. Robert had put a tape in and they talked about how great it would be when Toney wheeled in the parking lot on his last day at Hermitage.

Toney slowly hit his hand brake, like he had practiced, and stopped for a light, waiting to turn left onto the very road where he had crashed.

When the light turned green Toney began turning the wheel. Suddenly, as if the devil was pulling his arm, Toney's paralyzed hand slipped from the quad knob. The sensitive wheel spun completely left and the van rammed into a stopped school bus.

Steam was coming from the engine and the front left side of the van was completely smashed in. Toney leaned his head on the wheel and cried uncontrollably. He had failed in doing the thing that was going to save him. He had wrecked his dream.

PHOTO ALBUM

Toney, captain of the wrestling team.

A match begins.

Working for the pin.

The pin.

Crossing the finish line.

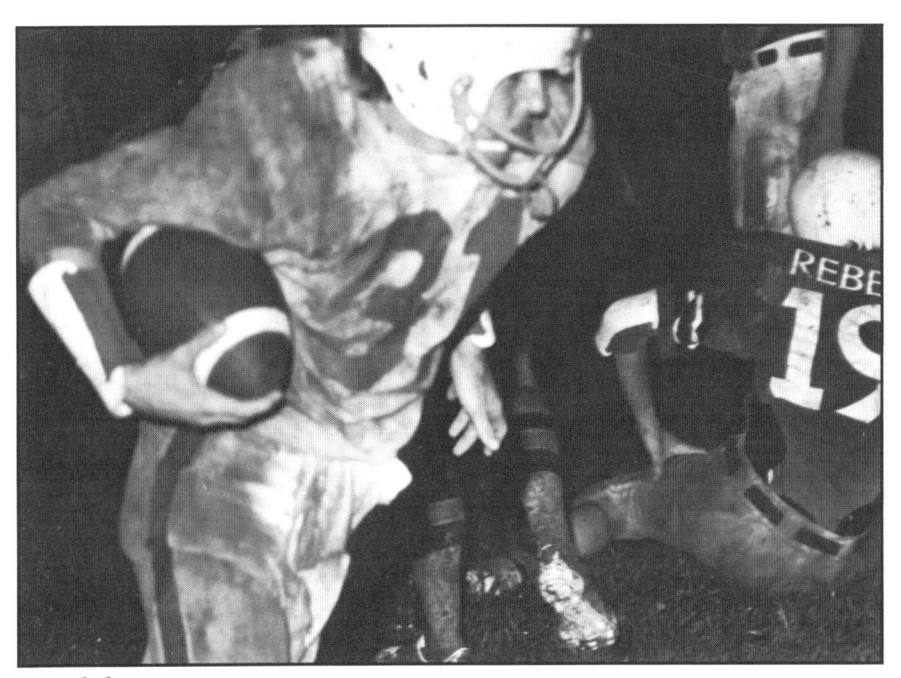

Touchdown.

108 The Toney Lineberry Story

"The car of my dreams."

Dreams demolished.

TWICE A CHAMPION 109

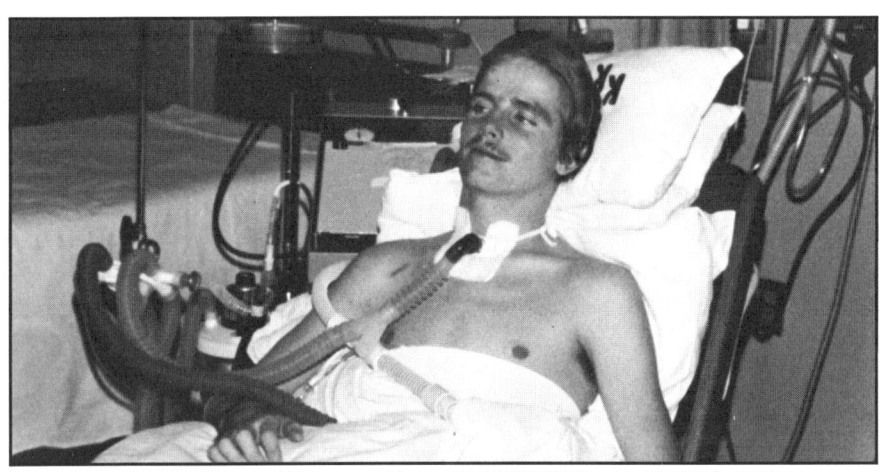

The respirator keeps Toney alive. "PPCHCH . . . PPCHCH"

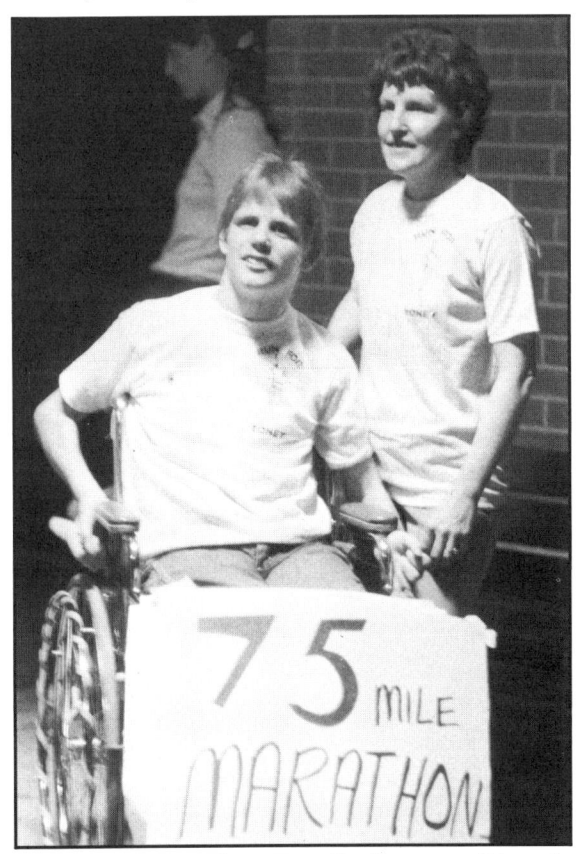

Toney and his mother, Eva look on as Hermitage cross-country runners and coach Donahue completed a 75 mile run to raise money for the Toney Lineberry Fund.

Working for the Virginia State Police.

Toney and Sgt. Pennington.

TWICE A CHAMPION

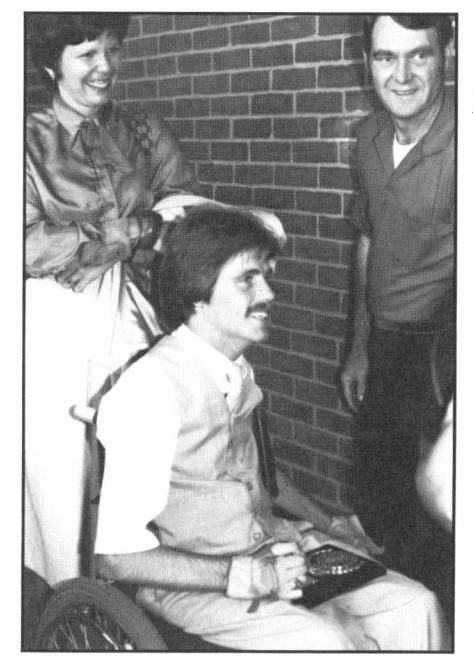

Rehabilitant of the year.

Toney plays with his niece, Kendall Koehler.

Danny catches a big one. Tommy's impression of Toney.

112   *The Toney Lineberry Story*

Toney enjoys reading, skiing, sailing, and other activities.

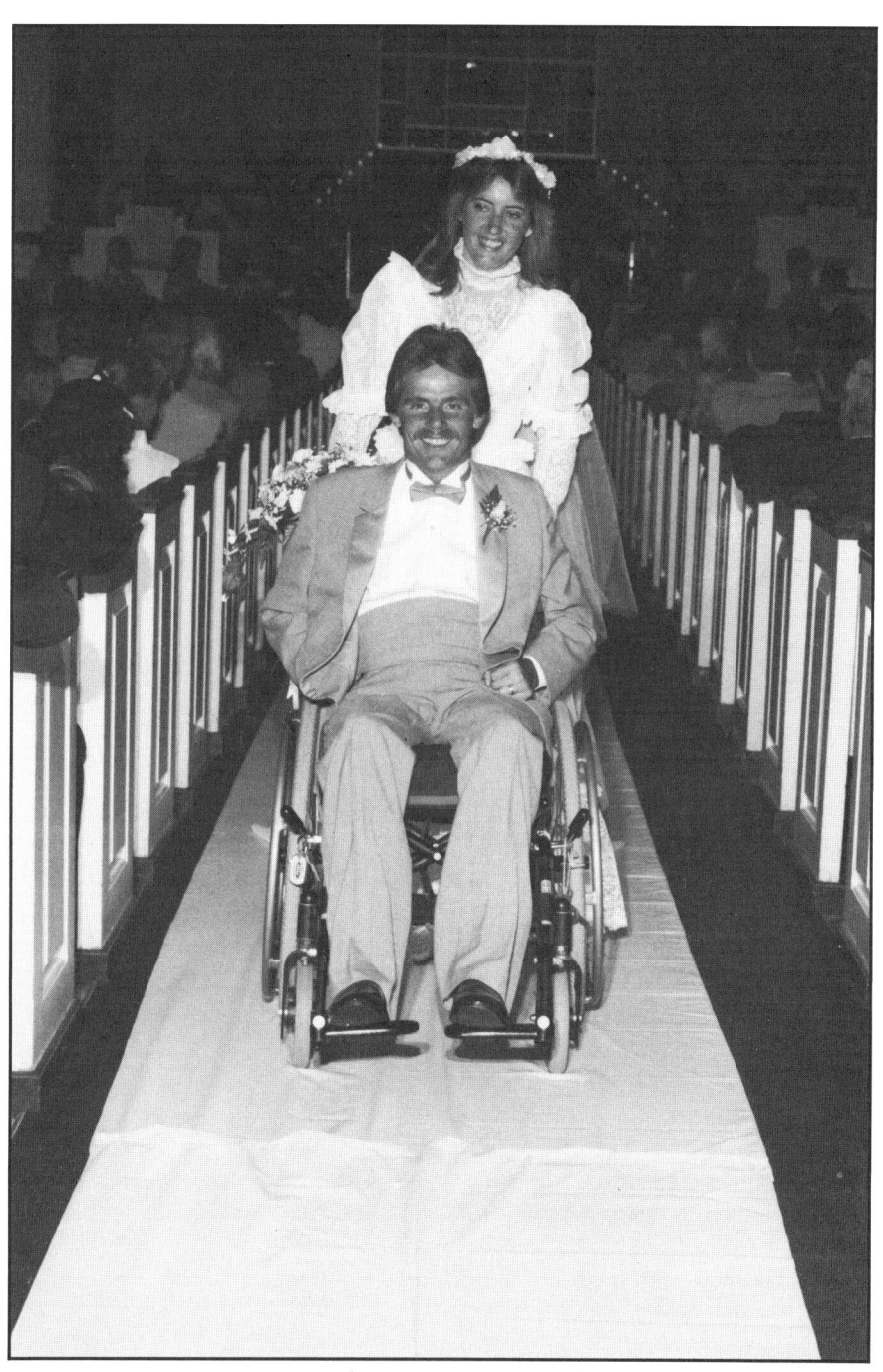

Mr. and Mrs. Toney Lineberry.

114   *The Toney Lineberry Story*

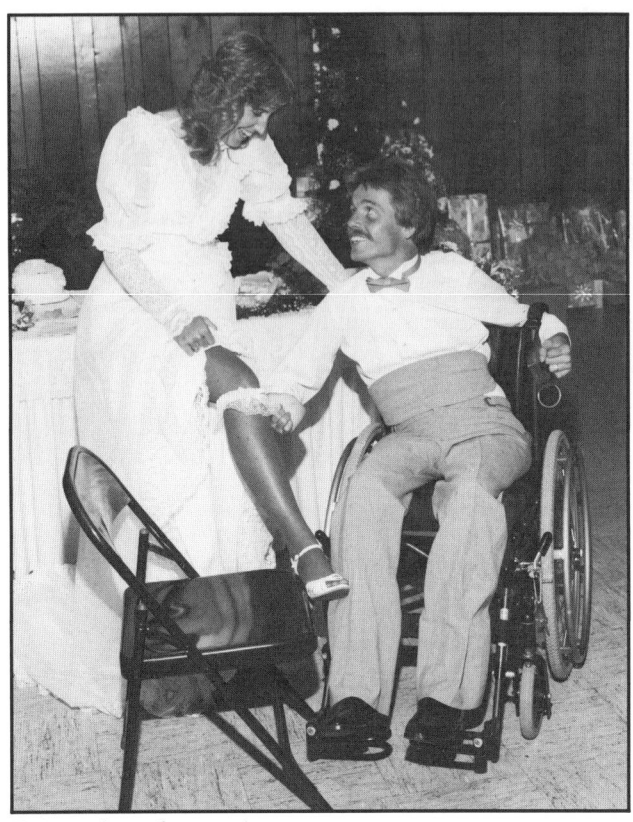

Removing the garter.

The wedding party.

Toney and Donna's home in Goochland, Virginia.

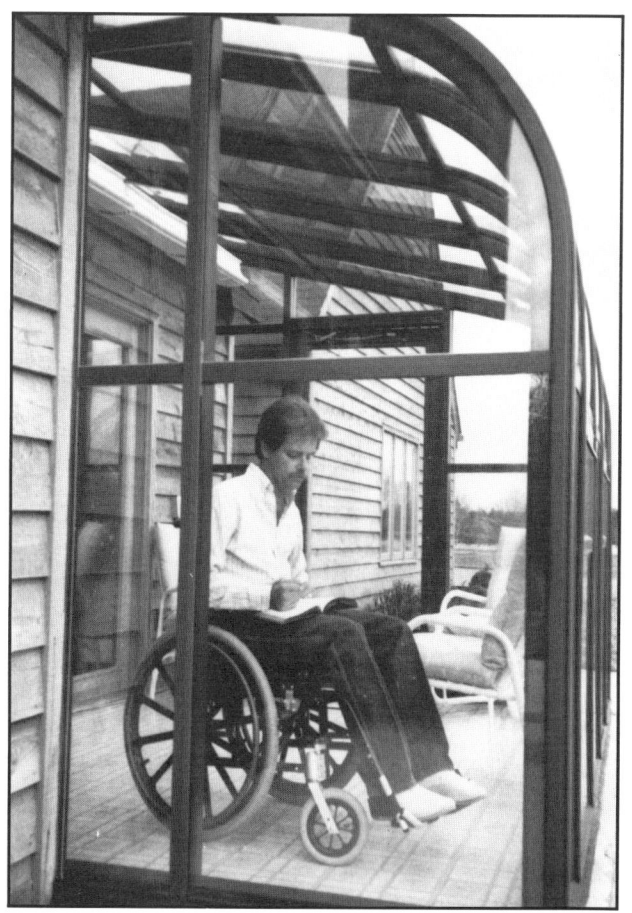

Toney reads in the sun room.

116   The Toney Lineberry Story

Mom, Dad, Donna and Toney.

Toney and the Schools family: C.B., Terry, and Jacob.

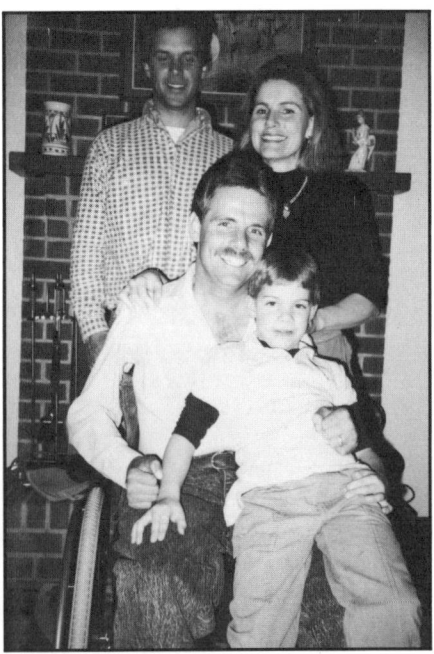

Toney and the Jackson family: Tate, Cathy, Jennifer and Tatum.

Toney and the Koehler family: Donna, Mike, Kendall and Mike, Jr.

Kyle Koehler gives Toney a kiss.

Donna, Toney and their nieces Kori and Kerry.

Toney and Virginia Governor, Gerald Baliles when Toney was presented "The Commissioner's Cup" for outstanding community service.

Toney talks with Walt Wilson and daddy after receiving the award.

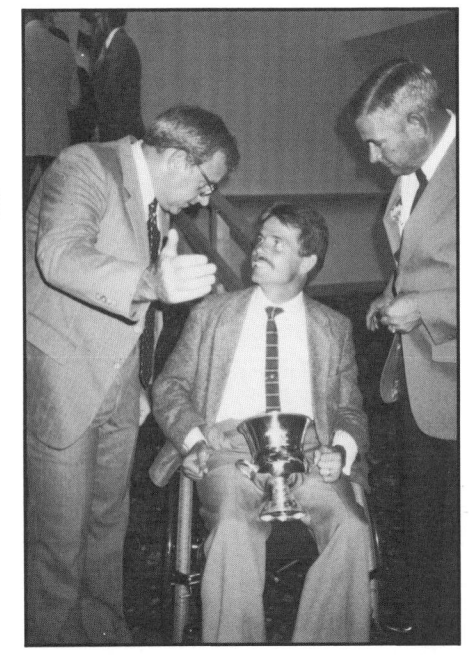

TWICE A CHAMPION 119

Toney and Donna with Elizabeth Dole, former U.S. Secretary of Transportation and Diane Steed, Administrator of the National Highway Traffic Safety Administration.

After receiving the Commissioner's Cup Award, Toney receives a lot of family support! Donna, Don, Eva, Mabel and Horace Brock, Pattie and Kevin McLaughlin, Cathy, Toney, Donna and Terry.

Toney plans a route before one of his many trips across the U.S.A.

Driving through California.

TWICE A CHAMPION 121

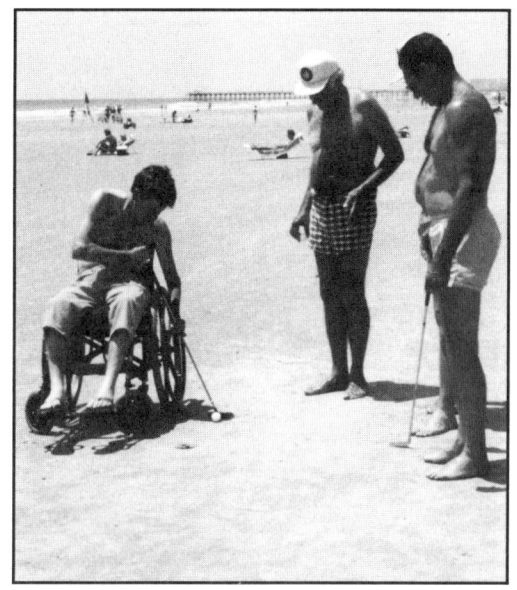

After many miles, it's time for a vacation.

Toney golfs at Myrtle Beach.

After a long day on the beach, Kevin, Toney, Tommy and Kenneth Luck relax in the jacuzzi.

The Toney Lineberry Story

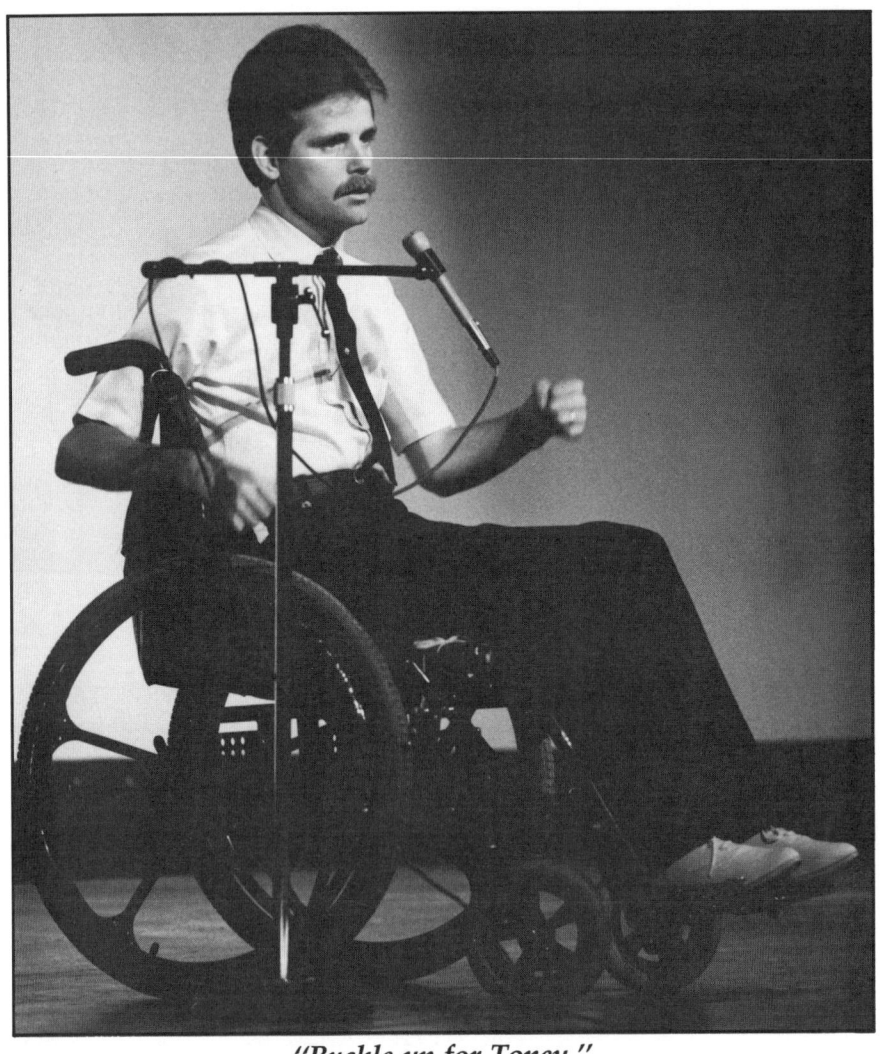

"Buckle up for Toney."

TWICE A CHAMPION 123

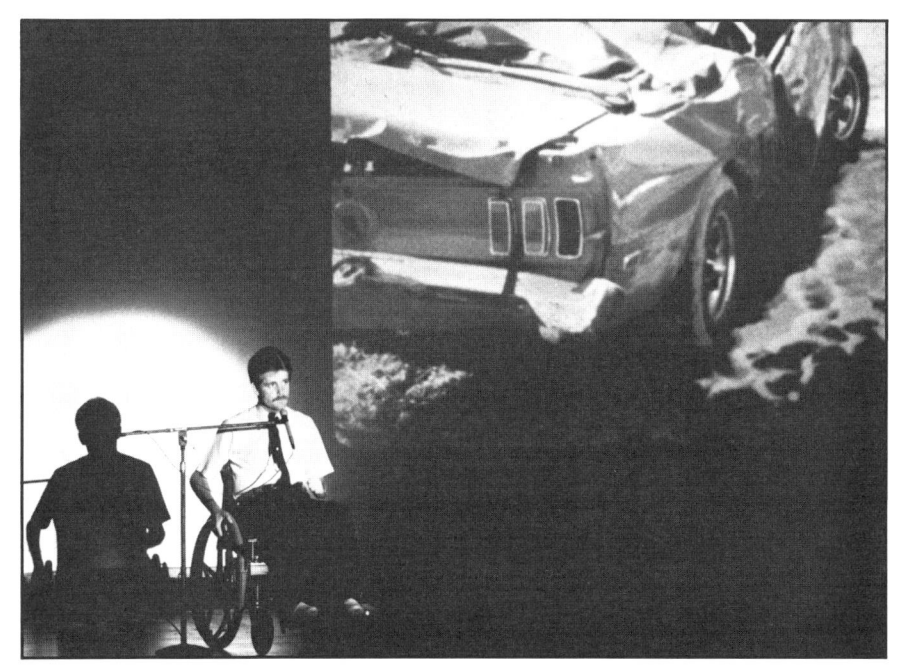

With all his heart, Toney shares his story with hope of saving lives.

CHAPTER 8
SO, WHAT ARE YOU GONNA DO NOW?

"I can't seem to do anything right anymore."

Toney sulked as he sat in our driveway watching his van being towed to the body shop. He was angry at himself. He was angry at his van. He was angry at the world. Just when he thought his life may somehow be coming back together, he crashed his van and was right back where he started. He was scared. He didn't know if he would ever have the courage to drive again. He pounded the wheel of his chair with his paralyzed fist. He was scared.

That was an awful day for Toney. All he could think about was smashing into that school bus. As he ate dinner that night, he decided he had to stop thinking about it. He was going to graduate the next day. It was the greatest accomplishment of his life. Although he had just experienced one of the biggest disappointments of his life, nothing was going to destroy his spirits for graduation.

Making it through high school was perhaps the most important thing Toney had ever done. For the first time since his accident he had a feeling that everything was going to be alright. "Maybe my life is coming back together."

There would be parts of high school that Toney would miss. He would miss the hundreds of friends he had made. He would miss the days when it was actually fun. Most of all, he would miss that purpose in life, that reason for getting up in the mornings. He was excited about the graduation night activities, but he was worried about having to answer that inevitable question that all graduates get. "So, what are you gonna do now?"

Toney was frightened by that question. He thought driving was the answer to his future. Now he was terrified of that van. He decided to forget about it and just enjoy his big day.

Graduation afternoon came and we were all as proud as can be. To us, Toney may as well have won an Academy Award, climbed Mount Rushmore, or flown to the moon.

The house was lined with balloons. You could feel the excitement in the air. We got a big laugh when mama dressed Toney in his graduation gown. The gown was made for someone about 5 foot 7, but for Toney, sitting in a wheelchair, it barely covered his knees.

Robert arrived in the evening to take Toney, for the last time, to Hermitage. He wouldn't be graduating for another year, but the school allowed him to push Toney through the graduation line.

My family and I sat in the stands waiting for Toney's name to be called. We clapped as the I's and J's were called. We knew he would be soon. Then, as if a huge boom of light had been cast over the stadium, his name was called and the entire stadium jumped to its feet with a roar of applause. It was like electricity was buzzing through the stands. We hugged each other and chills came over my body as the principal put a diploma in Toney's lap.

Toney was flabbergasted. Here were two thousand people standing and clapping their hands, all for him. He looked up into those stands and saw all the people who had helped him come so far back from his injury. He looked up, into the sky, and thanked God for all those wonderful people.

As if that wasn't enough, when Robert turned Toney around to take his place among the graduates, they were standing and roaring, too. A tear ran from Toney's eye as one after another hugged him. Each hug instilled a memory he would never forget.

Terry, Donna, and Cathy had a party for Toney that night. There was no way his sisters were going to let that night go by. They were determined to make every second special.

With graduation came the tradition of heading for the beach.

Toney, Cathy, and Robert loaded up mom's car and headed for that sandy paradise.

All of Toney's graduation friends were there. Everyone was determined he would have a normal graduation week at the beach. As everyone was getting sand between their toes, Toney was getting sand between the treads of his tires. He must have rolled up and down the boardwalk a hundred times.

When not on the beach, Toney and his friends sat on the hotel balcony and yelled at the girls walking by. He hadn't felt that human, that normal, in a very long time.

Toney came home from the beach and reality set in. That awful question came rushing at him like a freight train. "So, what are you gonna do now?"

He didn't know what he was going to do. He sat in his room one day and went over his options. He heard "As the World Turns" playing in the other room. He decided he could stay home the rest of his life and watch soap operas. No one would be too disappointed in him. After all, he had graduated. What else could he do?

Just then he looked out into the driveway and saw his newly fixed van. He was scared to death of that thing. It seemed to have failure written all over it.

The van sat in the driveway for weeks and Toney became an expert on "As the World Turns."

One day he decided he couldn't take it anymore.

"There's no way I'm sitting in this house the rest of my life!"

He went to mama and daddy and told them he would like to try to drive again. They had been saying all along that he should have proper training before trying to drive. This time he agreed. After all, how many crashes would it take before he learned?

So it was settled. Toney would learn how to drive. He was anxious and optimistic. Some day he would drive safely and things would be great. One big obstacle stood in his way, however: another stay at Woodrow Wilson. Toney didn't want to do it, but it was the closest place to get proper training.

The scene was familiar. Daddy drove Toney up the long,

asphalt driveway to Woodrow Wilson Rehabilitation Center.

Toney's stomach curled as he went past his old room. "What in the world am I doing here?" he thought.

The place seemed different this time. It wasn't quite as bad. There wasn't as much complaining and moaning going on. There weren't those long, tedious days of exercise. Toney wasn't the new kid anymore. He was a veteran and he was actually glad to be there. He wasn't there because he had to be. He was there because he wanted to drive, and he was determined that he would do it.

Woodrow Wilson is blessed with some talented people. They set Toney's van up safely. They adjusted it so Toney was more comfortable behind the wheel. Before, he always seemed to be reaching and straining.

Toney's first lesson was a long one. He became very tired before the day was over. He hoped it wouldn't always be this difficult.

That lesson involved two things. First, he would roll under the wheel, relax, and push the button for the power lock-down. This device locks the driver's wheelchair in a safe position.

Second, and this part took most of the day, Toney learned to reach and buckle his safety belt. He must have put it on a thousand times that day. It felt funny: he had never done it before.

With each lesson Toney learned more. Roll under, lock in, buckle up and a new skill would be learned. Toney would find himself asleep at nights dreaming roll under, lock in, buckle up, check brakes, relax, turn key. He did this over and over, for days and days. He became good at it and could do it by himself, with no struggle.

Toney still went home every weekend, but weekdays at Woodrow weren't so bad. When he wasn't in driving class he would sit, content, knowing he was accomplishing something.

One afternoon, Toney sat out on that same patio where he had spent so many days. He saw a paraplegic drive up, get out of his van, and roll into the building. Toney smiled. He knew he would do that some day.

Just then Toney got a familiar pat on his back. It was Walt Wilson, his friend and former counselor.

"What are you doing back here, buddy?"

"I'm gonna learn to drive, Walt. It's all I want. I'm gonna do it."

"I bet you will!" Walt patted him on the back again and went into the building. Toney felt like a winner.

Weeks went by and Toney began driving the van around an obstacle course. His teacher constantly coached him and she never let up. She pointed out his good points and his faults. He became a perfect obstacle course driver.

A big day came. Toney had earned his learner's permit and he was about to hit the open highway. He was very nervous, but he couldn't let it show. He had to prove to his teacher, and to himself, that he could do it.

He tooled slowly down the long driveway as if he was still on the obstacle course. He turned onto the highway and putted along for a few yards.

"Give it some gas, it's o.k.," his teacher encouraged.

Toney gave it some gas, and then some more, and before long he was doing the speed limit, tooling down Route 250 in Waynesboro with a wide grin on his face. He was not only driving, he was in control. He was as safe as anybody on the highway and he knew it. He had climbed one of the biggest mountains of his life.

Toney spent day after day driving those hilly roads. He became confident and downright good at driving. It was fun—he felt like he was at an amusement park every time he got behind the wheel. Days became routine as he and his teacher drove around Waynesboro. His arms would be a bit tired when they returned, but that would go away. He felt good.

One afternoon, Toney pulled into a handicapped parking space in front of the patio. His teacher watched as he rolled onto his lift and got out of the van. Two boys and a girl sat up on the patio and watched. They must have been thinking "I'll be like that someday."

Toney wanted to go up to them so bad. He wanted to tell them "it gets better, just give it some time."

I woke up on a frosty autumn morning and got dressed. As I laced my Nikes, I thought about the day ahead of me. Daddy and I were going to Woodrow Wilson to get Toney. He was to try for his driver's license that day. I couldn't believe it. My brother, my hero, was actually going to drive again. My whole life I thought Toney could do anything. After all this time of struggle, I knew once again that he could do anything.

We got to Woodrow and Toney was already on the road trying for his license. We waited for what seemed like hours until Toney pulled in. You could almost hear him smiling. He hurried to get out of the van and we ran over to hug him. I saw something moist in daddy's eye as he hugged his son.

The teacher told daddy that Toney had done as well as anybody she had ever taught. He was the most severely injured person to ever drive away from Woodrow Wilson at that time.

Daddy followed and I rode with Toney as we headed for Goochland. I sat on my knees in the seat without a care in the world. He drove home like he had been doing it all his life. He had gotten the proper training this time and he was as safe as anybody on the highway.

Our family was thrilled about Toney's accomplishment. Mama was so proud. She would get him to drive her to the store even when she didn't need anything.

Toney loved driving people places. He liked driving Donna to the grocery store. He would sit in his van playing with his nephew, little Mike, while Donna shopped.

I loved it when Toney picked me up from baseball practice. I never felt as proud as when my teammates watched me climb into his van.

Driving people places made Toney feel like he was helping somebody, instead of the other way around. Whenever somebody needed a ride, Toney was always the first to offer.

Things were fine and Toney felt good about himself. Then a friend asked "so, what are you gonna do now?"

Toney wondered if he would ever stop hearing that question. He thought and thought. He decided he had to do something.

He decided on college. A local community college was handicap accessible and Toney knew he could handle it. He wondered if he really wanted to go to school again, but the thought kept coming over and over: "I've gotta do something."

Our sister, Cathy, was the old college pro and she went with Toney to register. She helped him pick his courses and assured him he'd love it.

Toney's first day at college was a struggle. He was alone. His friends from high school weren't there anymore. He had trouble carrying his books. He had trouble writing fast enough to keep up with the professor. He struggled through it, though. He decided he would stick out this term no matter what.

Toney loved driving. He would drive for hours with no destination, happy as can be. There was one drive, however, that he didn't like. It was the drive back and forth to college. Each day he was forced to drive past the junior high, over a hill, and down through the gully where that near-deadly sheet of ice was that once flung him through the air. He had awful nightmares of his blue van bouncing off a pine-tree and down into that ravine. He began driving ten miles out of his way to avoid that stretch of pavement.

A problem was creeping up on Toney that he never anticipated. Before his accident he had a strong, powerful body. After it, he became very thin. As he got better he was told to begin eating more so he would get bigger. Now all of a sudden, he was getting too big. His body got no exercise and weight was gained easily. He couldn't just run it off like he used to. He decided it wasn't fair for mama to have to lift that extra weight as she got him out of bed. He began dieting. He was determined to get to a normal weight.

The community college term went on and Toney got into a routine.

One morning he pulled into a handicapped parking space and got ready to go to his first class. After unbuckling his safety belt, Toney reached for the button to open his door and he toppled to the floor.

"What in the world am I going to do now?" He was terrified

that he would have to lay there for days.

Through some miracle, Toney managed to reach up and hit the button to open his door. He lay there for hours yelling and screaming at everyone who walked by. Some people just went on by. Others went by pointing and laughing. They must of thought he was drunk or something. I suppose he did look it. Finally, a construction worker walked towards the van.

"Hey mister," Toney yelled.

"What happened fellow?"

"Uh, I'm paralyzed and I fell out of my wheelchair. Could you please help me?"

The big, burly construction worker helped Toney into his chair. Toney thanked him and apologized.

He looked at his clock. He had missed his class. He searched his mind for something that would make him feel better. He smiled. He knew that something lived on Irisdale Ave.

Our sister Donna lived on Irisdale. Toney cried as he told her what had happened. Donna squeezed Toney lovingly, just like she had done in a hospital so many times before.

Little Mike stood in the passenger's seat, wearing "Sesame Street" pajamas. He gave Toney a smile that no one could look at without smiling back.

The next day Mike Sr. showed up at the community college. He said he was just passing through, and he might as well help Toney in while he was there.

It didn't take Toney long to figure out Donna was behind that.

Toney drew strength from a thought: "It feels so good to know that I have a family that really cares for me. I know they'll never let me down."

Community college was going well, but Toney decided he wanted more. He wasn't the type to sit in school. He wanted to get out in the world and see what was waiting for him. He figured the best way would be to get a job.

But he didn't know what kind of job he wanted. All he knew was that he wanted to be happy, and he wouldn't settle for anything else.

It was tough finding a job. Handicapped people are probably the most eager workers in the world, but ample opportunities aren't out there. There are lots of businesses out there that could accommodate someone in a wheelchair if they would just make a few adjustments. I guarantee they would get a hard worker.

Toney searched high and low and was getting discouraged. One afternoon an old school buddy called with a job offer. The buddy was "Boo" Baird, a "Chevy Chase" sort of fellow. Boo worked for the Henrico County Recreation Department. He asked Toney if he wanted to help run a gym for kids during the afternoon. Toney was thrilled. He loved kids and knew Boo would be a lot of fun to work with.

Before beginning the job, Toney and Boo had to attend a meeting with the county supervisors to go over the rules and duties of the job.

The meeting was downtown, in a very hilly section of Richmond. Toney parked on the street and rolled onto his lift to get out of the van. As he swung the lift out and down, he and Boo talked.

When the lift came down to street level Toney backed off of it. Boo was reaching inside to get their things and didn't see him backing off.

Suddenly, the hill turned into a roller coaster. Toney went rolling down 27th Street, picking up speed, yelling "whoa . . . whoa . . . Boo . . . Boo!"

At the end of the road was the James River. Boo was sprinting for all he was worth. He knew Toney couldn't swim.

Before Boo could get there, Toney's chair hit the curb, flipped over, and sent Toney sprawling to the sidewalk.

Boo caught up with Toney. He saw his paralyzed body twisted into an "8" on the sidewalk. "Oh God man! What should I do?"

"Pick me up and put me in my chair."

Boo got Toney into his chair and they went into the meeting. Toney sat there, his hair looking like a bird's nest, his shirt torn, blood dripping from his elbow.

Boo just looked at Toney. He chuckled. "If he can handle that," he thought, "He can definitely handle this job."

Working at the gym wasn't like a job. Toney and Boo sat there laughing and watching kids bounce basketballs up and down the court. They would sit there, eating toasted bologna and cheese sandwiches and playing backgammon, remembering the good old days.

Toney loved being with those kids. They would ask him why he was in a wheelchair, and he'd tell them flat out. "I was in a car accident. A car is a dangerous thing and you have to be careful." The thought that those kids might remember that made Toney feel good.

The job at the gym left Toney with a lot of time on his hands. One morning, he decided he would drive up to Woodrow Wilson and visit. As he drove up the driveway, he couldn't believe he was actually going there because he wanted to.

Inside, Toney was greeted warmly. Everyone was real happy about how well he was doing. He got lots of hugs and things didn't seem gloomy there at all. He was smiling and laughing. This wasn't such a bad place.

Then Toney saw two very unhappy quadriplegics sitting at a table in the cafeteria. He felt bad for them and wished he could help them. He wanted so bad to go over to them and say "it's going to be alright. Things will get better."

Toney went outside feeling lucky. He knew what those people were going through.

On the way to his van Toney saw Walt Wilson. Walt seemed especially glad to see Toney. He was the head of the Spinal Cord Injury Prevention Project at Woodrow. He was starting a program where people in Toney's situation speak to groups about what had happened to them. He asked Toney if he would like to be a part of it.

Toney thought for a minute. He thought about those kids at the gym and how good it made him feel to talk to them. He thought about those patients in the cafeteria and how he wanted so bad to talk to them. "You know, Walt, I would like to help."

Toney's first assignment was speaking at a juvenile home for troubled teenagers. He drove across a bridge in Richmond and wondered what he was going to say to the kids.

Walt was waiting for Toney when he pulled into the correctional center. He told Toney just to tell his story and his situation now. "These kids may learn something," Walt said.

Toney felt a little nervous as he rolled in front of the kids. As soon as he began to talk, however, he started to feel at ease.

The kids sat silent and listened to Toney tell his story. He told of his wrestling days. He told how he disobeyed his parents and took the car. You could see some of the kids squirming in their seats. It was obvious that they could relate to the story. He talked about his accident. It was so quiet. You could hear the heater buzzing as Toney described his crash.

Toney shocked some kids that night. He made them think.

Toney soon realized that he liked being in front of people. He knew he had a powerful story to tell. He told Walt he wanted to speak more.

Toney's accident was a painful thing for him to think about. It really hurt to remember the details of that awful day. But if it meant preventing someone else from going through it, it was worth it.

It would be weeks before Toney told his story again. During that time he spent hours in front of a mirror practicing what he would say. He couldn't stop thinking that he could actually help people just by telling his story.

The fact that Toney was no longer in the hospital didn't mean that he no longer had therapy. He would never escape that word. He couldn't let his bones become brittle. He still needed muscle in his paralyzed limbs. Having a therapist exercise his arms and legs was very important.

He went to St. Luke's Hospital three times a week for therapy. Each time he pulled into the parking lot he wondered how mama and daddy must have felt on that cold January night that changed their lives.

Toney would often lie on a mat and lift weights with other patients. He became friends with a gentleman named Sumpter

Priddy. Mr. Priddy was a delightful man. He suffered from a disease that left his legs paralyzed. He would lie there and notice how hard Toney worked. They talked and Toney told him his story. Mr. Priddy gained strength from it.

"If he can handle this, then surely I can," Mr. Priddy thought.

Mr. Priddy admired Toney's courage and determination. He knew Toney was looking for full-time work, so he arranged an interview for him with the Virginia State Police.

Toney was very grateful to Mr. Priddy for getting him the chance. He longed for permanent employment. He longed to be productive again. He was grateful, but he was very nervous at the thought of taking on such a challenge.

As he drove to the interview, he wondered if he could handle it. He thought nervously about what might be asked or expected of him. He desperately hoped that he could handle the job. He wanted it so bad.

As Toney pulled into the parking lot at the state police headquarters, it overwhelmed him. There was a huge, brick building. Police cars were lined up in front. Gigantic American and Virginia flags hung from a very tall pole, flapping in the wind. Everything looked so official, so in order. The way Toney's life once was. The way he longed for it to be again.

Toney got out of his van and slowly, one revolution at a time, pushed himself up a ramp and down a long sidewalk towards the building. When he was almost there, he stopped in his tracks and noticed two flights of big, concrete steps, the kind that seem to engulf wheelchairs.

Huffing and puffing from the long trudge, Toney's head drooped. "How can I work at a place like this?"

Just then a duty sergeant came out and helped Toney up the steps. The man was very nice and the steps weren't a problem that day. But Toney wondered what he would do if he got a job.

Inside, Toney was given a formal interview. He remembered all the things he had been taught at Woodrow Wilson about handling yourself in public. He remembered being told to have tact, not to be bitter. He handled the interview very well. He did something he was getting good at: he made the interviewer forget about his wheelchair.

The man was obviously impressed with Toney. "We have a few positions available. Why don't you come back in a week and we'll see what we can do."

Toney was thrilled. He couldn't wait to get home and tell daddy the news.

When Toney told him about the job, daddy's ears turned red and seemed to wiggle with excitement. He took his "John Deere" cap off and then put it back on. With all the love in the world he said "you're making it, boy."

Mama got home and hugged Toney after she heard the news. Toney felt ten feet tall as she leaned over and squeezed him. He wanted so much to make his parents proud. They had relieved so much of his pain. He wanted desperately to repay them.

Toney drove to the headquarters once again, but this time in a very optimistic frame of mind. He was ready to take on the world.

The steps were still there when he arrived, but the same duty sergeant was waiting for him.

There were two positions available. The first was in the mail room. The head of the department showed Toney all he would have to do.

"You've got to lift this, lift that. You've got to put this over there."

Suddenly, Toney was not ready to take on the world. He looked at his balled up, paralyzed fist. A bad feeling swam around in his stomach. He looked at the man and said, apologetically, "I don't think I'll be able to lift anything."

There was one more hope. A position was open in criminal records. Toney was introduced to Kitty Galli, the department supervisor. She gave him a caring smile and welcomed him. She assured him if there was anything he couldn't do, they would work it out. From that moment on, Toney knew he was in good hands.

The job went well. The people in Toney's office did all they could to help him. They helped him with his lunch and even sharpened his pencil for him.

Toney didn't need much help. He filed and prepared records to be mailed. He worked hard and was downright productive. He had found a niche. He felt like a winner.

Each weekday Toney drove to work and put in his eight hours. The steps weren't a problem anymore. The people at the headquarters built a ramp just for him. Each afternoon he rolled down it to his van.

He fought the rush hour traffic on his way home. He felt normal.

Almost every afternoon Toney would drive by our sister Donna's house on the way home. Some days she would wash his hair for him. Some days she would straighten his necktie. Some days she would just sit in his van and listen to him. No matter what the weather, she never complained about coming out to his van.

One winter morning Toney pulled up in front of Donna's house. He honked his horn, like he usually did. Slowly, her door began to open. Little Mike poked his head around the screen. He smiled at Toney and went darting down the steps. He tiptoed across the cold grass, his stubby little legs only covered by "Spiderman" underwear, and climbed into Toney's van. They played games until Donna came running out after him.

Toney was speaking more and more. He seized every opportunity to tell people that there is life after tragedy. He told people how much he regretted that icy night.

Toney was asked to return to Towers Hospital and speak to some of the patients there. He accepted gladly. He remembered how he felt when he was there. The thought that he could perhaps make some people feel better overwhelmed him.

Toney felt great as he pulled into the parking lot at Towers. He felt strong and powerful as he came to a place where he was once weak and puny.

Toney really helped some of the patients. "You'll be alright," he would tell them. "Time is the best healer."

These people saw that Toney had gotten away from Towers

and that he was driving. Some of them realized that they could do it, too.

Toney developed a very normal social life. His wheelchair still caused problems, but he was learning to deal with them more and more. He still had bad days, but doesn't everybody?

His social life centered around his friends. Every weekend night, he and his friends would hit the town. I would sit on the sofa and wonder where he was going all those nights. I was too young to realize how many girls were out there.

One night all of Toney's friends were busy. He was determined to go out. He didn't want to sit at home. He wanted to be with other people. He decided to go out alone.

He drove to a nightclub that he and his friends visited often. He could hear the music thumping inside as he drove past the bar's big, heavy door. He wondered how he would get in.

Toney sat in his van trying to figure out how he was going to get himself into the bar. Then a friend from school came up to the van. He was a bouncer at the bar and asked Toney if he needed any help.

Toney had learned to gladly accept help. As far as he had made it back, he knew he hadn't done it alone.

"Thanks man, I appreciate it." The bouncer rolled him towards the door.

Meanwhile, a beautiful girl in a red dress was sitting inside. She was at her usual table, with her friends, right by the dance floor.

A strobe light periodically traced her face. A fan blew a breeze through her hair. She sat there laughing with her friends, saving two seats for some friends who were coming later.

A bouncer came up to the girl's table. "My friend's in a wheelchair. Would you mind if he sits at your table so he can see the dance floor?"

"O.K., I guess so," the girl said hesitantly.

The bouncer went to get Toney. The girl sat there thinking. "Great! I've sat here all this time to save seats for my friends and they're going to bring some guy in a wheelchair over to our table!"

Then Toney rolled to the table. The girl recognized him from school. She didn't know him personally, but she remembered how touched everyone had been by his accident. She started to feel better about giving up the space at her table.

Toney was introduced to everyone. He immediately noticed the girl in the red dress.

"I'm Donna, Donna Brock. I remember you from Brookland."

Toney talked to Donna, and everyone else at the table, for the rest of the night. He felt good that he had gotten out on his own and met new people.

He felt especially good about meeting Donna. At the time, he thought she was dating someone else, but he knew he wanted to see her again.

Donna and her friends didn't mind the intrusion at all. They thought Toney was good looking and that he was very personable. He talked to them and made them forget his wheelchair.

As time passed, Toney saw Donna several times at the bar. They talked a lot and they began liking each other very much. Their personalities seemed to match.

Toney liked Donna more than he had any girl since his accident. He was, however, very hesitant to fall for her. He had learned to be very cautious.

To Toney's surprise, Donna asked him over for dinner.

"Do you live on the first floor?" Toney asked.

Donna laughed and said yes.

They had dinner and Toney was pleasantly full as he rolled himself away from the table. He smiled and thought what a great cook Donna was.

They watched T.V. and Donna held Toney's hand. She hadn't thought about his wheelchair since the night they met. She was falling for him.

As Toney buckled himself into his van, Donna stood in the doorway. "I'm dying to kiss you," she whispered.

"Then why don't you?"

They kissed and Toney used all the biceps he had to put his arm around her. Chills came over him. He felt like he never had before. He was falling for her.

Toney spent many more evenings at Donna's apartment. They began to date and Toney really seemed happy. He had dated other girls, but he hadn't felt like this in a long time.

Toney loved his job. The people at the State Police were great. They all helped as much as they could. They seemed interested in his situation.

He made that long drive to work everyday. He would never go straight there or straight home, however. He would always make it a point to visit someone. Whether it was stopping by a sister's house, watching me at baseball practice, or going by Donna's apartment, he always visited someone. He remembered those long, painful days in all those hospitals. He remembered how it made him breathe just a little easier when people visited him. He never wanted to lose that breath of life that his friends and family had given him.

Toney's boss, Kitty, would do anything for him. She was so understanding. She was just one more person who made Toney feel special. She was one more person who made him realize that he was going to make it.

Kitty knew how much Toney loved speaking to groups. She knew how important it was to him to tell his story. She would gladly give him a day off to give a program.

The more Toney told his story, the more he thought about his accident. He constantly went over it in his mind. He wanted to remember every detail. He desperately wanted to figure out what had happened to him.

One day, while looking through some safety literature at the police headquarters, he came across a report on how safety belts work.

The report described how the lap belt keeps the driver in front of the wheel, where he can possibly control the vehicle. Toney remembered being slammed from the left to the right. He remembered how that sheet of ice took control of the car.

The report described how the shoulder harness catches the passenger and locks him in the seat. Toney remembered being slammed into the dash and windshield. He remembered a steering wheel being wrapped around his neck. He remembered spitting glass. He remembered trying to move his body, and not being able to.

Mostly Toney remembered a safety belt slapping him in his face as his car tumbled into that ravine. He stared at a picture of a mannequin being caught by a safety belt.

In disgust he thought, "this could have been prevented."

CHAPTER 9
BUCKLE UP FOR TONEY

Toney became obsessed with safety belts. He thought about them constantly. He studied them tenaciously. He had one taken apart for him so he could see exactly how they worked. He would sit in his van and hurl himself forward as the shoulder harness caught him every time. He would pound the steering wheel with his paralyzed fist. He was convinced that that simple strap could have prevented all his pain and suffering.

Toney didn't stop with the thought that the belt could have saved him. He decided that he would add this new-found knowledge to his program. He was determined to spread the word that the simple click of a safety belt can save your life.

Toney's first and toughest task was getting his friends and family, the people he cared about most, to buckle up.

One afternoon, Toney was to drive me and mama to our sister Donna's house for dinner. As we took our seats in the blue Ford van, he made an unusual request.

"How 'bout putting on your selt belt, mom?"

Mama was puzzled. She had never worn the belt before. She looked at Toney, who spoke before she had a chance to reply.

"I've been studying them and I've realized that I might be walking if I'd only worn mine. Can you believe it? If I had only buckled that belt, it might have made the difference."

Toney's voice cracked as he asked mama to buckle up for him. I never saw her in a car without a safety belt on again.

That became Toney's theme. Each time he came in contact with a friend or family member near a vehicle he would ask them to buckle up for him.

Toney sat in his buddy Danny's driveway, behind the wheel of his van. Danny stood by the window, spitting tobacco juice now and then, as they talked.

"Do you wear your safety belt?" Toney asked.

"Never really thought about it," Danny replied.

"You know, we'd probably be jogging right now if I'd put mine on. That thing can save you, man."

Danny put his head down and thought for a second. As the green bill of his cap rose, he mumbled "You're right." Danny began buckling his safety belt. He thought of Toney with every click.

Eventually, Toney persuaded all his family and friends to buckle up—for him. It seems that the biggest reason many people don't buckle up is that they just can't remember. We always remember because we hear Toney's voice asking us to do it—for him.

Toney's story was very powerful. People would often remember what he had to say and remember to buckle up. As more and more people buckled up for Toney he began to feel special. He was touching people's hearts. He was so sincere, carefully telling his audiences about the day and night of his accident and how a safety belt could have saved him.

He would leave the programs with a great feeling in his stomach. He thought that if just one person buckled up, his time on stage had been worthwhile. It was the way he used to feel after scoring a touchdown or pinning a wrestling opponent. He never thought he would have that feeling again.

A great demand was forming for Toney's talks. He was beginning to need countless hours away from work to present his program. The people at the State Police were super. They realized the great service Toney was doing, and they decided it was more important than his clerical work.

Toney's life began molding into shape. He had a steady job with steady pay. He also had his programs. He had a chance that not many people get, the chance to save lives. Preventing people from going through what he went through meant more to him than anything.

Something else was beginning to become very important to Toney. It was a very strange feeling, but for the first time in a long while he was beginning to have strong feelings for a girl.

Donna Brock wasn't just any girl. She was beautiful and she was perfect for Toney. They were right for each other. They had the same hobbies. They liked the same music. They were both very close to their families. They both wanted the same things from life. And, more than anything else, they loved each other.

Their relationship was very, very normal. Toney's wheelchair meant nothing to Donna. She was in love with Toney, and nothing else mattered. He realized this and it strengthened his love for her even more.

He realized she felt this way, but he wondered how her family would feel. He was very apprehensive about meeting them. Would they approve of her dating a man in a wheelchair? How could he ever take care of her?

One night Toney and Donna were out to dinner. Donna mentioned that her parents were at a nearby lounge and she asked Toney if he would like to meet them. He was hesitant, but he knew how important Donna's family was to her. He knew if he was to keep seeing her he would have to meet them.

Horace and Mabel Brock immediately shook Toney's hand. Just like their daughter, they didn't seem to notice or care about his wheelchair. Toney felt like he had known them for a long while.

As the four of them talked the night away, Toney decided he had found a very special girl who had a very special family.

I remember when Toney first brought Donna out to our house. She seemed to bounce right up to the door. It was as if I'd known her all my life. We all fell in love with her immediately.

They were going for a ride that day and they asked me to come along. I sat in the back seat, beside Toney's wheelchair, drinking a cold Nehi bellywasher, watching as Donna drove with one hand and held Toney's paralyzed fist with the other.

It was only a ride in the country, but from the look in their eyes you would have thought they were on a two week Caribbean cruise. I knew something was going on. Toney seemed so happy and so content. It was great.

Toney sat on the deck of our Goochland County home on a chilly autumn day, a streak of shade tracing his face. The afternoon sun kept him warm, however, as he thought about the path his life had taken.

He remembered winning wrestling match after match and the path he thought his life would follow. He remembered gasping in an ambulance, thinking he would die and that his path had ended. He remembered sitting in a rehabilitation hospital thinking his path couldn't be much longer.

Now Toney believed his path was only beginning. He had overcome the talk that he would never drive. He had become partially independent. He had built a social life, with a myriad of friends who saw him and not his chair with wheels. He had met the girl of his dreams and acquired a feeling in his heart he never imagined possible. The words "Buckle up for Toney" were being heard all over the state of Virginia. His pain and suffering was beginning to help people.

Toney had a future. Millions of doors that he thought would always be impassable could now be opened.

Toney took a deep breath and realized that his counselors at Woodrow Wilson were right. Time *does* heal all wounds. And handicapped people *can* live normal and productive lives. This feeling overcame Toney as he thought about what his future could hold. He decided to go for it.

Toney thought of how he could spread his message to a greater number of people. He was speaking to community groups, churches, and high school groups on a voluntary basis. The Virginia Department of Motor Vehicles was constantly in touch with him and helped him set up many programs within the state. This was great, but Toney wanted more. He wanted to reach a different group of people and different types of people. He decided to go for the top, the National Highway Traffic Safety Administration (NHTSA).

Toney sat behind the table in our den for countless nights after work. With a pen propped between his fingers, in a scribbly handwriting, he wrote "Buckle Up For Toney, A Proposal That Can Make a Difference." The proposal told his story, how he wanted to tell it to others, and how he hoped they would buckle up—for him.

He sent the proposal to NHTSA and set up a meeting with Ms. Diane Steed, the deputy administrator of the administration.

Toney was so excited. It was as if he was about to meet the President of the United States. He was to speak to a powerful government agency, an agency committed to highway safety. He had a very good feeling that they would be receptive to his proposal.

While Toney was excited, he was also apprehensive. It would not be a casual speech to a group of high school students. It would be a tense, sophisticated discussion with a panel of safety experts.

Toney slept little the night before his big trip to Washington D.C. It was quite a challenge for him. He had never driven that far alone before and he didn't know what the nation's capital had in store for him.

Mama got Toney up at 5:30 a.m. He buckled himself into his blue Ford van and was on his way.

Interstate 95 rumbled with traffic. Toney's heart pumped with anticipation as he headed for D.C. He became a bit more at ease, because a friend from work had arranged for her dad, 1st Sergeant Dennis Robertson, who was stationed with the State Police in Northern Virginia, to meet him just outside of D.C. and escort him into the city. This is a prime example of how supportive the people with the State Police were. They allowed no obstacle to stand in his way.

As Toney maneuvered through the maze of roadways in central Washington he shook his head, wondering what in the world he was doing there.

He pulled up to the Department of Transportation building and just stopped and looked. It was huge. It had the typical government look.

A security guard showed Toney to a parking space, and he

rolled inside. He was on his way to the elevator when he stopped at the end of a hall, in front of a picture of President Reagan. He looked up into the sincere eyes of his president. He drew in a firm breath and wheeled his chair down the hall.

You could have heard a pin drop in that NHTSA conference room that day. Toney spilled his story out to them. He told them he just wished he would have had sense enough to buckle up that night. He told them he knew some people would buckle up if they could hear his story.

Diane Steed was impressed. She asked Toney to travel with her the following Monday to Baltimore where she would speak to four hundred drivers education teachers. Toney was honored. He looked forward to the chance to hear her speak.

Toney drove Ms. Steed to Baltimore. It was another distance record, the longest journey he had made in his van. On the way, he pulled off the interstate to get a drink out of his cooler. Ms. Steed was filled with compassion as she helped Toney wrap his fingers around the Mountain Dew can. She knew she had met a very special person.

Ms. Steed was very dynamic as she told the drivers education teachers how important their job was. Toney sat calmly and watched her end her speech. She finished by saying "and now I would like to bring a special friend up to tell you his story."

Toney's stomach filled with knots. He had no idea she was going to do that. He was overwhelmed. He had never spoken to that many people before.

As Ms. Steed held the microphone to his mouth, he told the teachers his story. He told them how he remembered sitting in a class like theirs and thinking "it'll never happen to me." A hush gripped the audience as he said "but now I know that it can happen to me again, it can happen to anyone in my family, and it can happen to any of you out there." He ended his spontaneous speech by encouraging the teachers to tell their students that "sometimes when you think you've really got it made, you need to slow down and take a second look at things."

The crowd jumped to its feet and let out a roar. Ms. Steed was standing, too, grinning from ear to ear. The press surrounded Toney. The *Baltimore Sun* wanted an interview and Washington's channel 5 had a camera rolling.

This was great. People were recognizing what Toney was doing and actually hearing his message. He was as high as he had ever been. He had an incredible feeling that there was no stopping him now.

While driving Ms. Steed back to Washington Toney couldn't stop thinking about that feeling. He dreamed of reaching that many people with his program everyday.

Then another very strong feeling overcame Toney. He felt his stomach tighten as he thought "wow, look at me now. I can't believe this! I just spoke to four hundred people. I'm driving the deputy administrator of the National Highway Traffic Safety Administration back to Washington D.C. I can't believe this! I must be dreaming!"

It was not a dream. Ms. Steed praised Toney's speaking ability as they puttered through the D.C. traffic.

One of the best days in Toney's life was about to end. Toney didn't know that it would become even better before it was over.

"How would you like to go to Arizona?" Ms. Steed asked as they entered the parking garage.

Before he could answer, she continued, "It would be for a week. You would speak to the National Association of Governors Highway Safety Representatives."

Toney was overwhelmed. His face locked in a grin as the excitement seemed to take his breath away. He almost peeped out "me?" But instead, as if he'd been doing this for years, he answered, "That would be great, Diane. I've always wanted to see that part of the country. And I think it would be a great opportunity to reach a lot of people."

Diane was outsmiling Toney. "I'll call you soon to make the arrangements."

On the way out of D.C. Toney experienced his first traffic jam. It took him hours to move a few blocks. He couldn't believe it. Cars were snorting and coughing. People were cleaning their windows, reading books and newspapers. He felt sorry for those who looked like they had grown used to it.

Toney had an incredible feeling on his way home. Suddenly, he felt more powerful, more independent, than he had since his accident. Chills came over him. He felt like he could do anything.

He was hungry. He saw a McDonalds and his feeling of independence overcame him. He decided there was no reason why he couldn't stop and eat by himself. He had overcome tougher obstacles.

As he weaved through the drive-thru lane, Toney remembered how many times he had barked out an order from his Mustang . . . "Give me two cheeseburgers, a large order of fries, and a Pepsi!"

This time he slowly hit the button to roll down his electric window. He ordered a plain fish sandwich.

Toney drove up to the window. He had a five-dollar bill propped between his fingers. He carefully handed it to the lady at the window. She took the money and reached out to hand him his food.

As a whiff of the fish sandwich drifted under his nose, Toney remembered that his paralyzed hands would not allow him to clutch it.

He didn't get discouraged.

"My hands are paralyzed," Toney explained. "Could you please help me?"

The lady was very nice, like most people when they realize Toney's situation. She told him to pull up and that she would bring it to him.

It was the best sandwich Toney had ever eaten. He felt like he had really grown on this day. There was nothing he couldn't do now.

Toney couldn't wait to get home and tell everyone the news. He was on cloud one hundred and nine. Finally, good things were starting to happen to him.

The next morning Toney sat out on the deck of our house. He remembered thinking "go for it." He smiled as he thought that he went for it and it paid off.

Toney was nervous about the Arizona trip. When he thought about it in detail he wondered "Who will take care of me? How does a person in a wheelchair get on and off an airplane?"

Mama made him feel better by saying that she would gladly sacrifice a week from work to go to sunny Arizona with him. Toney decided there would be many good people to take care of him and he stopped worrying.

I had never seen Toney as excited as he was on the morning they were to leave for Arizona. As he was about to put a spoonful of cornflakes into his mouth he put the spoon down. He seemed to gaze into space. He looked so proud. Nothing could stop him now.

I drove mama and Toney to Byrd Airport. We were running a little late and we grew apprehensive as a red light caught us just as we reached the airport.

Just then the feeling that "nothing can stop me now" vanished. The smell of urine drifted through the air. I sighed as Toney screamed that his leg bag had busted.

"OH NO! NOT NOW! We're gonna miss the plane!" Toney was hysterical.

Mama, as calm as a Sunday morning, put her hand on Toney's shoulder. "It's O.K. We'll just have to fix it, that's all."

I stood guard as mama changed Toney's pants and leg bag in the airport parking lot. It just goes to show that even when you think things are going great, bad things can still happen. You just need to be prepared and deal with them. My family was learning that. Oh how my family was learning that.

We still had seven minutes as we hurried Toney into the airport for the first and biggest flight of his life. He was about to find out how people in wheelchairs get on and off an airplane.

Toney was immediately transferred from his chair into an "aisle" chair, a light, skinny chair designed to get the passenger to his seat.

The attendants handled Toney roughly. I suppose they were used to handling luggage.

Toney's wheelchair had a tag attached to it and was shipped away with the suitcases and other luggage.

As Toney was wheeled through the security gate, he heard a familiar voice behind him.

Cathy pleaded with the guards that she was late and would they please let her go hug her brother. They wouldn't, and she threw a candy bar over the fence to Toney as he headed for the plane. She waved and yelled "goodbye and be careful!"

Toney saw Cathy at the viewing window as he boarded the plane. She wiped a tear, as if he were going to some far away place.

I stood beside Cathy with my arm around her. I knew our brother would be fine. I knew he would be a winner in Arizona, just like he had been everywhere else.

Toney was on his way. On his way to giving the biggest speech of his life. He looked out of the airplane window and remembered playing with matchbox cars as he saw a highway below. He wished life could be that simple again.

When the plane landed in Arizona representatives from the NHTSA were waiting for Toney and mama. They drove to the hotel-resort where the conference would be held and both Toney and mama's mouths dropped open. The place was huge and beautiful. They were very excited to be staying in such a place.

But once inside, the excitement died down a bit. Toney's supposedly wheelchair accessible room wasn't accessible at all. He had come all this way to speak to all these people and he couldn't get under the bathroom sink. He sighed and wished hotel builders would consult the handicapped before building.

But, as always, they made do. Mama went out and bought a rubber dishpan to use as a makeshift sink so Toney could wash his hair, brush his teeth, and shave.

Toney was very happy to be there. He gazed out the balcony window and hoped the governors' representatives would believe in what he had to say.

There was standing room only in the resort auditorium. A buzz of whispers moved through the audience as Toney nervously rolled about backstage.

He said one final prayer as he was being introduced. He then slowly rolled onto stage, decked out in a blue three-piece suit. Mama stood in the corridor, proud as a mother-peacock.

Toney began his speech. "My name is Toney, Toney Lineberry. I'd like to take you back to a time in my life that was very important to me."

Toney went on to talk of his childhood, his football, his wrestling, his car. He then described that very memorable day.

"I remember me and my little brother listening to the D.J. on the radio waiting to see if our schools would be closed."

He told of mama and daddy coming home telling stories about the weather conditions. He told of his fight with mom and dad, his conversation with his friend, and of sneaking the car away. During the speech, slides of Toney's Mustang flashed in the background.

Toney's voice began to crack. He talked softer and his tone was lower as he described the body of water that was flowing across the road. A tear formed in his eye as he recalled "but it was not water at all, it was a solid sheet of ice."

OOOHS and AAAhs came from the audience as a slide of Toney's mangled Mustang flashed on the screen behind him. Some people cried as Toney chokingly admitted "I'll never walk again."

He went on to describe how a lap belt might have held him in place, in front of the steering wheel, in control of the automobile. His voice cracked as he explained that a shoulder harness, that simple shoulder harness, might have prevented him from being thrown into the steering wheel, the dash, and the windshield; how it might have prevented him from breaking his neck.

He finished his speech by grabbing the audience's heart one last time. "If you can't buckle up for yourself, or for your friends and family, which are really all the right reasons, then maybe, just maybe . . . maybe you can buckle up for me."

Hundreds of people fell in love with Toney that day. It was the most emotional, most dynamic speech he had ever given. His heart felt like it was going to pound through his chest as the audience gave him a standing ovation. He grinned as he thought "I could get used to this."

Toney spent the rest of the week making friends and speaking to smaller groups. Several of the governors' representatives told him they hoped to have him come to their states someday. Toney told them he'd love to, thinking how incredible it would be to see more of the country.

You would have thought the Queen of England was arriving as Toney and mama's plane landed in Richmond. Me, my family, Donna, Danny, Boo, and several other friends of Toney's waited at the gate and shouted "welcome homes" as he rolled towards us. Donna squeezed him so hard I thought he was going to fall out of the rickety airline wheelchair.

You could sense how proud everyone was as we had a party for Toney back at the house. He was so excited that he couldn't eat. He and mama told us about the trip.

Toney's confidence grew and grew. The nervousness that he used to have before speaking slowly began to disappear. This was because he was learning more about highway safety. He became confident in the message he was trying to get across.

Toney made countless friends across the state. Letters were constantly sent to his supervisors at the Virginia State Police. The messages read like "We heartily support Mr. Lineberry's safety presentations and are proud of his efforts."

Toney was persuading many people to buckle up. Safety was a very, very important part of his life. He loved the idea of helping people by making them safer.

But he also wanted to help another group of people. These people were not interested in automobile safety. They were interested in where their life would take them next. They were in a situation Toney knew a great deal about. They were newly injured spinal cord patients.

Toney joined the Virginia Community Cadre Network, a group of spinal cord injured persons who volunteered to assist newly injured persons when they return home. This meant a lot to

TWICE A CHAMPION

Toney. He remembered how frightened he was when he was first hurt. He remembered wondering if his life was over. He was determined that he would help some people conquer these fears.

Toney had developed a full life. It seemed that he was always either talking with newly injured patients, traveling the state giving his program, or socializing either with Donna or some of his friends.

Toney continued to speak to the patients at Towers. He never forgot that he had the chance to help others get through a time that was so painful for him.

At Towers Toney was befriended by Mark Andrews, a recreation counselor there. He heard Toney speak of his athletic days, and he thought Toney may be interested in a program he had started.

"How would you like to go skiing?" Mark asked Toney after a very inspiring program.

"What? You mean snow skiing? How?"

"Sure, snow skiing! We'll fix up a sled for you to ride in. It's safe. You'll love it."

After a little thought, Toney decided to give it a try. It seemed a challenge to him. And he had never turned down a challenge before.

Mark didn't tell Toney at the time that he would be the first quadriplegic to ever attempt skiing in Virginia.

When he arrived at the snowy mountain in Massanutten, Va., Toney saw Mark unloading the sled that he would ride in. As he looked at the sled he remembered swooshing down a snowy hill when he was a kid. He remembered getting scarred up as he fell off the sleigh. He remembered getting snow down his pants. He remembered tracking muddy snow on mama's freshly waxed kitchen floor. He remembered how fun it was. A rush came over him as he thought of the chance to do it again.

It was hardly apparent who was under the mass of clothing that hid Toney's quadriplegic body. A red helmet and goggles covered his face. A chin strap clutched his chin. Lift tickets hung from the zipper on his heavy jacket, flapping in the cold wind.

His paralyzed legs felt nothing. They were zipped into a sleeping bag, sitting, contented, on the floor of Toney's toboggan.

The toboggan had a large back rest and a roll bar. Toney was strapped in tight, with crisscrossing safety belts, like a baby in a child safety seat.

A Toney smile peeked through his helmet as the sleigh went slowly up the ski lift.

His body shook. He didn't know if he was nervous or if the cold rattled through his veins. It didn't matter.

Mark would tether behind Toney, with ropes attached to the sleigh to guide it. Toney would lean from side to side, partially guiding the sleigh.

Toney soared down the beginner slope, the wind whistling through his helmet. He let out a boyish "whoop" for joy. He was a kid again.

Toney skied the whole day. He felt so alive. He was actually participating in a sport again. He would fly down that mountain and forget about being paralyzed.

During one "swoosh," Toney was picking up more speed than ever. As he hit a divot in the snow, the sled flew through the air. Toney let out a screech as memories of a red Mustang raced through his mind. The sled rolled violently over and over. There was nothing the attached skier could do to stop it.

The sleigh finally skidded to a stop. The safety belt helped Toney's body remain unscarred, but his face was a waterfall of blood.

Mark ran to him screaming "Are you alright?"

Toney pulled into our driveway. I almost cried when I saw his face. It was just one big scab.

"What happened?" I demanded as I helped him off his lift.

"I just took a little tumble. I'm o.k."

"Tough day, huh?" I tried to make him feel better.

"No, it was great. I'm going back next week."

That "little" crash didn't phase Toney. The scars on his face were worth the chance to play in the snow once again.

Toney also enjoyed a less adventurous form of recreation. He began finding pleasure in, of all things, books. He hated reading in school. He saw no purpose in it, and only did it when it meant passing.

Toney now saw a lot of things differently. He saw life differently. He saw reading as a new form of recreation well suited for someone in his condition. He saw reading as a chance to give him some of the knowledge he had cheated himself out of in school.

It all started with the reading of safety pamphlets, books and magazines. He would read anything connected to automobile safety in hopes of passing on the information in his program. But he slowly began reading other things. Donna bought him two books on the Civil War. He immediately read them both cover to cover.

He became fascinated with the war. He remembered grandma telling him stories about our ancestors fighting in it. He remembered sitting on her knee savoring her every story, her every word. He wished he had carried that same enthusiasm into the classroom.

But now he was making up for it. He read book after book on the war. It amazed him that so much history had occurred right in his hometown. He would sit up late at night, slowly turning pages with his clenched fist, as mama stretched out on the couch waiting to help him to bed.

Toney's travels took him throughout the state of Virginia. This gave him the opportunity to visit many Civil War battle sites. Mama would pack him a bologna sandwich and a cooler and he would just sit in his van at the sites. He would often get frustrated because he couldn't actually get out and walk up to sites, but he could still read the historical markers.

Over time, Toney read more and more about the war. He began to learn in great detail about its meaning and its consequences. He eventually became an expert on it. He was proud to be a "son of the South," but he realized what the war was all about. He felt that two separate countries would have been awful for our land.

Toney would often share his knowledge with Donna as she accompanied him to battlefield parks. This would give him the chance to get a closer look as she pushed him right up to the sites. Most Civil War sites are hilly, with very rough terrain. It was often very hot, and Donna often struggled getting Toney where he wanted to go. She never complained, however. She would pack a picnic lunch and they would fall deeper and deeper in love with every trip.

Toney and Donna were becoming an item. He spent hours at her apartment and she began traveling with him to his programs whenever possible.

Donna is a very assertive girl. She knows what she wants and she seems to always get it. And she wanted Toney. She is also organized and always in control, qualities which he shared and greatly admired. She is also beautiful, which didn't hurt either.

Donna made Toney very happy. She somehow made his life full again. I rarely saw him down.

Bad things still happened, though. His leg bag could still burst or there could still be a flight of stairs he couldn't get up. But these problems were becoming easier and easier to deal with. With the help of a lot of people, Toney was slowly learning to live with his handicap. He remembered thinking he would never be able to do that.

We all knew Toney had come a long way back. I smiled as I sat on the sofa in our wood-paneled den. I thought about what great strides Toney and our family had made to win this long, awful battle.

I was proud of us all. My sisters were all married and had wonderful lives.

I was a junior at Goochland High School and had overcome that time in a kid's life when he doesn't feel like he belongs, when he wonders what he's doing on this earth. I overcame it while watching my brother almost die, then fight to regain his life.

I was proud of my parents, who struggled both physically and financially to prevent Toney's death. They were still in rough financial shape, but seemed as happy as ever.

I was proud of us all, but oh how I was proud of Toney. Before, he was always my hero. I admired his athletic accomplishments and the way he dominated life.

There was no longer anything athletic about him. And he no longer dominated a room. But now he spread a zest for life, and a zest for other people's lives. He didn't just care about trophies or himself. To me, that meant more than all the wrestling titles in the world. He was still my hero.

As we sat at an awards banquet at Woodrow Wilson, we found out that a lot of other people had recognized Toney's comeback. My family, Diane Steed, and some friends from the State Police and DMV sat with Toney at a table as Walt Wilson began to speak.

"Ladies and Gentlemen, it is an honor for me to have the privilege of presenting the Virginia Rehabilitant of the Year to you at this banquet."

Mama knew that Walt had nominated Toney for the award, but no one knew if he would win it.

The microphone squeaked as Walt continued to speak.

"This award, sponsored by the Virginia Rehabilitation Association, is given to a disabled person who was successfully rehabilitated in the past year. The nomination committee, in making their selection, bases their decision upon:

—the person's rehabilitation gain;
—acceptance of his or her disability;
—employment;
—and contributions that the person makes to society."

There was no question that Toney had fulfilled these criteria. Our table turned into one gigantic smile as Walt continued.

"The person who is the recipient of this award had an automobile accident, leaving him with a spinal cord injury and being quadriplegic. He was eighteen-years-old at the time of injury, captain of his high school wrestling team, and enjoying his high school activities like most average teenagers."

We all knew Walt was talking about Toney. We looked at him as he squirmed in his chair, about to blush.

Walt went on to describe Toney's rehabilitation, his employment, and his accomplishments. He then read some comments from people who had nominated him for the award.

From a supervisor at the State Police: "He shows enthusiasm in his work as well as many outside activities. He is an inspiration to the other employees. Toney's password has been 'I'll try' on all assignments, and so far he has never failed. With his disposition, attitude and determination, I don't think he ever will."

From a former rehabilitation counselor: "Working with hundreds of vocationally handicapped over a ten-year period had produced many personal and professional rewards for me. Out of that experience Toney has been the biggest inspiration for me to continue in the saddle. Give me a Toney every ten years, or maybe every fifteen, and I will never get off track."

From a patient at the Towers who was present during one of Toney's visits: "His recent visit was gratifying and enlightening for all of us here. His combination of empathy, courage and, most importantly, achievement has proven a lasting boost to our spirits and hopes."

Walt's words seemed more intense and sincere as he had a comment of his own.

"Those of us who have had the privilege to know this young man and to work with him have been truly amazed at his dedication to not only performing his job well but also his almost ceaseless drive to educate others about spinal cord injury, trying to prevent other young people from suffering this injury. He is truly a role model, not only for other persons with spinal cord injury, but for *all of us*.

"Ladies and gentlemen, it is a tremendous pleasure for me to present to you the Virginia Rehabilitant of the Year, Mr. Toney Lineberry."

It took Toney a long time to roll himself to the podium. His head drooped. A tear of happiness dripped from his eye as Walt put a plaque in his lap.

Toney was not at a loss for words. His eyes seemed to gleam.

"I don't know if I deserve this. There are so many people out there who should be standing up here with me. I thank God for my family and friends who have allowed me to come so far back. I never could have done it alone."

CHAPTER 10
A FULL LIFE

They scamper about, scraping, scuffling, laughing, crying. They throw rocks and they throw kisses. They know less about people, but perhaps more. They don't know the endless struggle for money and prestige. They don't know the hustle, bustle, and problems of the world. But they know love. Oh, how they know love.

Toney sat in our driveway, soaking up the warmth of the sun, feeling lucky. He felt lucky on this day not because of all he had achieved, not because of how far he had come back, but because of the two bundles of joy that wiggled under his wheelchair, as if it were a cover from enemy gunfire.

Little Mike, and an even littler Jake, took turns pretending Toney was their fort. He didn't mind. He even made explosion noises for them once in a while.

Toney spent every second he could with his nieces and nephews. They seemed to represent that breath of life, that slice of normal pie that he had craved for so long.

They didn't know what a broken neck was. They didn't know why Toney couldn't walk, and they didn't care. He was just uncle Toney.

Mama always cooked a Sunday meal. My sisters, their husbands, and their kids would come up every week to dig in to one of mama's masterpieces. My brothers-in-law and I would eat until we couldn't move. We would just groan away from the table.

But Toney would always eat lightly. He had put himself on a strict diet. At one time, he had gotten very heavy from sitting in that chair all the time. And he had too much pride for that. If he was going to speak in front of people, if he was going to open his heart to people, he had to look good. Otherwise, people wouldn't take him seriously.

Toney put himself on a rigorous exercise program. Part of the old "obsessed with being in shape" Toney was reappearing. Part of the "I will be a champion" Toney was evident.

He would roll himself back and forth through the shopping mall for hours at a time. He would lift wrist weights until nothing else was on T.V.—the screen just a pattern.

He remembered running miles and miles, never feeling weak. He remembered struggling on a mat in rehabilitation, hating it, and feeling very weak. Now he was somewhere in between, looking good and feeling good about himself.

Demand for Toney was tremendous. He began having to turn down speaking engagements because of his duties with the State Police.

This was something no one wanted, especially Toney. Toney's message was helping people. People were buckling up because of him. People were living because of him.

Toney was very grateful for his job in the department of records and statistics at the State Police, but it was evident that he was needed elsewhere. He was transferred to the Virginia Division of Motor Vehicles to give safety presentations full-time. This meant a lot to Toney. It meant that he could spread his message to more people. It meant that by working with very talented people, he would become even more schooled in highway safety.

Toney's last day with the State Police was a special one. They gave him a big party. He received lots of pats on the back, "I'll miss you's," and hugs. But most of all, he received more of the support that had gotten him where he was. They gave him a plaque for his desk—"Buckle Up For Toney." It would sit on his desk at DMV and remind him of his good friends at the State Police.

It would also remind him of his new main task, asking people to wear their safety belts.

Toney spent many evenings after work at Donna Brock's apartment. They loved being together. He always looked forward to seeing her.

His visits were average, yet special. They snuggled, watched T.V., laughed, ate, and snuggled some more. They enjoyed each other's company. Their relationship was normal.

But Toney's situation was not normal. Things needed to be done for him, embarrassing things. Toney was nervous when he first asked Donna to empty his leg bag. It was either ask her to do it or go home. He wanted to stay.

"I hate to ask you to do this . . ." Toney explained to Donna about the tube that he urinates through into the bag strapped to his leg. He asked her if she would empty it for him.

"Oh, I thought it was something like that," she replied. "I don't mind at all."

Nothing about Toney was a problem for Donna. She emptied his bag over and over. She pulled him up and down steps. She transferred him in and out of her car. She never complained.

Rain sprinkled Toney's windshield. His wipers screeched across the glass every few seconds. He sat behind the steering wheel, bundled up in a heavy coat and rain hat. Heat blasted from the vents.

Toney gave his horn a polite "honk" as he looked towards the door of Donna's apartment. He knew she would come bouncing out to see him any minute. She always did.

Donna scurried down the sidewalk, smiling in adoration as she headed for the shelter of the van. She jumped in, dripping from the rain, and gave Toney a big hug.

Toney began to have an incredible feeling. There was nothing this girl wouldn't, or couldn't, do for him. He thought back to how mama had devoted herself to him. He remembered how nothing was ever a problem for mama, how she never complained. Toney couldn't believe that he had found a girl that he could even begin to compare to mama.

Toney spent lots of time on the highway. His work with DMV took him all over the state. He had lots of time to think, about a lot of things. But these days, he mostly thought about Donna.

He was having feelings that he had never had before. He

thought about things that once seemed so impossible, but now were within his grasp. The more he thought about Donna, her every quality, the more he decided he loved her.

He remembered Donna saying it to him, but he couldn't say it back. He used to be so afraid of those three words. They had ended in pain in the past.

But now, as he drove down I-64, he couldn't wait to get to Donna's apartment to say those words to her.

Toney didn't even need to blow the horn as he pulled up at Crestwood Apartments. Donna was running down the sidewalk before he could put the van in park.

Donna immediately asked Toney how his program went. She was always interested. She believed in him. She had even begun wearing her safety belt because of him.

A serious look covered Toney's face. "There's something I've been wanting to tell you."

Donna's face drooped. She just knew Toney was going to say he didn't want to see her anymore. She drew in a firm breath and prepared herself for the worst.

Toney's serious look turned to one of affection. "I love you."

Donna dove over the seat into Toney's lap. She wrapped her arms around him and squeezed him. She kissed his cheek.

"I'm so happy," she whispered as he hugged her back.

The next day, Toney sent Donna flowers at work. She beamed as she showed them to her friends at the doctor's office where she was a bookkeeper.

But things were not always rosey. Toney occasionally had fears. He sometimes wondered if it was fair to "impose" his handicap on someone else. He wondered if anyone else could be as special as mama. He wondered if things would always not be a problem for Donna.

Over time, Donna proved that Toney's fears were unfounded. It became very obvious that her love was genuine.

They loved each other, and nothing else mattered, not a wheelchair, not a leg bag, nothing. There was no pity. Donna loved Toney the person, not Toney the quadriplegic.

Toney's love for Donna penetrated deeper and deeper into his heart. He knew he could never feel this much for anyone else. He decided he wanted to spend the rest of his life with her.

After his injury, Toney never thought he would get married. He never imagined he could find someone who loved him and who could deal with his injury. He found her, and she made him as happy as he had ever been.

Toney wanted to keep his engagement plans a secret. He wanted to go buy an engagement ring all on his own. He wasn't doing that great financially, but he cashed in some savings bonds for a down payment.

Toney pulled into the handicapped parking space at a jewelry store owned by a good friend of his named Brian Cowardin. He slowly got out of his van and rolled to the door. A smiling lady opened it for him.

Toney was very proud of the ring he had picked out. He sat in his van, just staring at it. As it glittered in his lap, he thought about the life he and Donna would spend together.

"I'll give her everything," he thought.

Toney gave a program at a local high school the next day. The ring was nestled in the backpack attached to his chair.

To Toney's delight, a student asked if he was married.

"Now that you mention it, I have something to show y'all."

Toney spent the next five minutes struggling to get the backpack in his lap and retrieving the ring.

He finally got the ring box out. The students were on the edge of their seats, necks stretching, waiting to see what it was.

"I've been dating this girl, and well . . ." Toney blushed as he spoke to the kids, "I'm gonna ask her to marry me."

He slowly opened the box and the ring appeared. "Ahhs" floated through the auditorium. The students jumped to their feet and applauded Toney's good news.

It was Toney's birthday. He asked Donna if she would have a party for him. He made a long list of guests and asked her to send invitations for him. The list included friends Toney hadn't seen in years.

As Donna was writing invitations, Toney asked her if she had pierced ears. She also had a birthday coming up, so this question made her think she would be getting earrings.

Toney told Donna he wanted his birthday to be special. He asked her to go to a Civil War battlefield park with him that afternoon. She was reluctant, because she needed to prepare for his party that night, but she knew how much it meant to him and she agreed.

Toney and Donna sat at Gainesmill Battlefield Park. The sunshine poured through the windshield of the van. Birds whistled from a nearby tree. Toney whistled in his heart as he and Donna talked.

"I've got a surprise for you."

"What?"

"Close your eyes."

Donna put her hands over her eyes, expecting earrings any minute.

Toney handed her a tiny box. A little smile formed over her mouth. She just knew she would love her new earrings.

When Donna opened the box, the sun swarmed over the diamond ring. It seemed to shoot sparkles as it glowed in the light. She began to cry. It was a happy cry, ringing with the kind of joy one only experiences a few times in their life.

"Will you marry me?" Toney softly asked. He knew what the answer would be, as she continued to cry and grin.

"Well? Will you?"

Donna took a deep breath, trying to control her joy. "Yes! Definitely!" She slipped into his lap and kissed him.

They stayed in each other's arms for a while. They talked about their future, and how happy they would be.

Toney told Donna that he knew he was ready to take on the responsibility of getting married. He believed that he could never feel like this again, and he knew that she would make him happy for the rest of his life.

Donna told Toney that she would do anything for him. She didn't have to tell him that his wheelchair meant nothing. He knew that. She sounded so in love as she told him how wonderful she felt.

The two happiest people in the world sat in a Ford van at Gainesmill. They couldn't wait to share their happy news with everyone. Toney planned to make the announcement at his party that night.

Daddy would be driving a Trailways bus that night. Toney wanted him to be the first to know, so he and Donna drove to the bus station when they left the battlefield park.

The smell of diesel fuel hung heavy at the bus terminal. Daddy was wrapped in a blue overcoat as he stood in the doorway of Toney's van.

"We've got some news for you, dad." Daddy had no idea how good this news would be.

"I asked Donna to marry me." Daddy's forehead wrinkled as he smiled. He put his arm around Donna.

"I'm real happy for you, son."

Daddy's words did not do justice to his feelings. Toney was always his pride and joy. He always had big dreams about Toney's future. There was a time, as daddy leaned over a hospital bed, that he thought those dreams had ended. Now, as Toney's life again became happy and full, the dreams were alive and well. His son had made it.

Toney made Donna promise she wouldn't tell anyone the news that day. He had a speech planned for his party that night.

I was the first to arrive at the party. I noticed Toney and Donna were especially happy. They hugged and kissed each other more than I had ever seen. I assumed they were just looking forward to the party.

It was a great party. With the exception of mama, who was home babysitting the grandchildren, and daddy, everyone Toney could have possibly wanted to be at the party was there.

Donna turned the music down. "O.K. everyone, Toney's gonna open his presents now."

Toney's lap was piled with packages. "I'm not much for making speeches, but before I open these I have a few things I want to say."

We were use to Toney's speeches, but we had no idea what he was about to announce.

Toney talked about what a special day it was, then shocked us all by saying "but it's not special because it's my birthday. Donna has made this day special for me."

The room was quiet. Toney paused to adjust one of his legs before he continued.

"I asked Donna to marry me today," Toney said, as my sisters screamed for joy in unison. "And she said yes."

Confetti should have been falling. I just kept hugging people. I finally pushed my way to Toney. I put my arm around his shoulder.

"Damn, I'm happy for you," I shouted to him over the happy chatter.

"Thanks, buddy." Toney gave me a big smile. "I want you to be a part of the wedding."

I was never as happy for Toney as I was that night. I had almost forgotten the misery he had endured in all those hospitals. I remember praying that he just not have any more pain. Now he was so happy.

It seemed that everyone in the world knew about Toney's engagement except mama. Toney wondered what her reaction would be as he and Donna drove to the house to tell her the next morning.

Mama's love and support had made Toney what he was. She completely gave herself to him when he needed her. For a long while, her life centered around him. He never could have made it without her. She was the woman in his life.

Toney knew mama would be overjoyed about the new woman in his life. She seemed to always thrive on his happiness. This would be a great day for her.

Toney now had two passions in his life, highway safety and Donna. As he traveled the state convincing people to buckle up, he carried his love for her with him.

Toney's travels for DMV were limited to the state of Virginia, but he still made some very long trips. On a cold morning in

February, he was scheduled to speak at Virginia Tech, a university four hours away.

The program was at 9:00 a.m., so Toney had to leave at 4:00 a.m. Mama had to begin getting him ready at 2:30. These were common mornings for Toney and mama. She never complained, though. She would do anything for her son.

At 5:05, Toney began his two hundred mile trip. It was dark. Fog floated in front of his headlights. Rain pelted his windshield. Very few cars were on the highway.

Toney was not intimidated by the circumstances. He thought back to his readings of the Civil War. Lee and Jackson must have faced much tougher situations.

The sun made an appearance as Toney neared Tech. He pulled over to rest his arms.

Before Toney could put the van in park, a state trooper pulled in behind him.

"Oh no," Toney thought.

The trooper walked up to Toney's window. "Are you alright, Toney?"

The trooper remembered Toney from his job with the force. His good friends were still looking out for him. They believed in what he was doing.

Toney gave an inspiring program at Virginia Tech. He spoke to a chapter of S.A.D.D. (Students Against Drunk Driving). He told them that he wholeheartedly supported their cause. He was for saving lives, no matter what the situation.

Toney explained that even though he wasn't drinking, his crash was alcohol related.

"I wouldn't have been going to that party if they had been serving Kool-aid and popsicles."

Toney made the long drive home, completing his fourteen hour day. He was scheduled to speak in Alexandria, Virginia, about three hours away, the next day. He didn't mind, though. The more people he could reach the better.

Toney's reputation was growing. His story was becoming very well known. He began getting requests to speak outside the borders of Virginia. His job with the Department of Motor Vehicles was to speak within the state. Toney had a strong desire to reach as many people as he could, wherever they were.

He was very grateful to DMV for the opportunity they had given him. They had schooled him in highway safety. While working with them, he became a very polished and professional speaker on the subject. DMV gave him security, a good stable job.

Toney had a decision to make. He wanted to reach people in other states, but this would mean leaving the security of his job. He would have to contract work on his own. It would be quite a challenge.

Before making a decision like this, Toney had to consult his new partner. He asked Donna what she thought about him going on his own.

Donna knew how much passion Toney had for his cause. She knew the risk her future husband would be taking if he left his job. She gave him her blessing.

Donna so believed in Toney, she decided that after they got married, she would leave her job also and travel with him. They were to be a team in every way.

Toney left DMV with their blessings. They knew he would be saving lives, wherever he was.

Toney had business cards printed. "Toney Lineberry: Professional Consultant on Highway Safety"

He modified a pamphlet that DMV had produced about him. The outside cover had a picture of Toney from the shoulders up with a serious look on his face. It read: "I never thought I'd be paralyzed at 18."

The inside cover displayed a picture of Toney in a wheelchair. It read: "Had I worn my safety belt I might be walking today."

The pamphlet briefly told Toney's story. It advertised his program. "I share my story with you in hopes of preventing people of all ages from experiencing the pain and misery my family and I have endured."

Big bold letters read: "Toney speaks nationwide."

Work did not pour in immediately for Toney, but he was

making it. He still spoke a lot in Virginia. He'd have a few programs in Maryland, North Carolina, and a few in Pennsylvania. He spoke to employees at Dupont, Phillip Morris, and Virginia Power. He stayed busy. Different people heard his story almost every day, which was the important thing.

Toney and Donna set a wedding date in September. When the end of summer rolled around, their nervousness began to appear. Donna made plans almost every day. She and her mother spent hours making arrangements.

Toney had a problem. A good problem. He had so many friends, so many people had been so important to him, so good to him, he couldn't decide who to have in his wedding. He chose twelve ushers, including daddy as his best man. Me, his three brothers-in-law, Donna's brothers, and some very close friends were included, but several others would feel left out. Toney hoped they would understand.

The sky was a vivid blue. Toney and Donna couldn't have asked for a more beautiful day for their wedding.

Mama dressed Toney in his tux that afternoon. They were both very happy. Toney smiled at his mom. He didn't have to tell her how much she meant to him. She knew, as she smiled back.

Toney drove, alone, to the church. He kept telling us that he wasn't nervous, but as he backed out of our driveway he almost hit a tree.

As Toney drove down the interstate towards the church his mind began to wander. He felt so proud. He was proud to be getting a girl as wonderful as Donna. He felt whole, like a fulfilled man.

Toney almost missed his exit as his nerves tightened.

Daddy eased Toney's nerves as they waited in the "grooms room" before the ceremony. They chatted with our cousin, Milton, who would perform the ceremony.

Hatcher Memorial Church was full. It was a good thing Toney had twelve ushers, as we escorted in five hundred people to witness his big day.

Toney's friend, Larry Hickman, videotaped the wedding. He

wanted Donna and Toney to have a film of this memory forever.

Toney sat proudly by the pulpit. We all gave him a smile as we marched past him to take our places in line. His friend Boo gave him a thumbs up. I winked as I walked by.

The sound of a trumpet drifted crisply through the church. It sent chills down Donna's spine as she and her father prepared to walk down the aisle.

Toney's face seemed to light up when she appeared. She had the cutest smile, as she clutched her father's arm.

They said their vows. They seemed so sincere, so in love, as they repeated Milton's words, gazing into each other's eyes.

The words "for better or for worse" seemed especially appropriate on this day. There was no question that these two could make it through anything.

"I now pronounce you man and wife."

After their first kiss as a married couple, Donna threw the train of her dress over her arm, put her bouquet in Toney's lap and pushed him down the aisle.

Toney and Donna were swarmed with best wishes at the reception. It was all very overwhelming. The whole day was like a dream. All of the kids, including my fellow ushers and me, had a ball decorating Toney's van for the honeymoon. It had to show the happiness of the couple inside.

Toney and Donna were pelted with rice as they headed for the van. Children formed a circle around Toney's wheelchair.

Donna gave all the children a balloon off the van before they left. Toney hugged them all. He loved them so much.

We all said our goodbyes. I saw happy tears form in mama's eyes as she hugged Toney. Daddy told his son how proud he was.

I shook Toney's balled up fist. He gave me a wink, as his lift hoisted him into the van.

Toney and Donna stopped at a car wash and then at a gas station on the way to their honeymoon. Donna signed the credit card ticket "Mrs. A. W. Lineberry." She told Toney how wonderful that felt.

They spent a week of love in the Pocono Mountains. The resort had a few barriers, but they handled it, just like they always would.

In the beginning, Toney and Donna lived with my mom and dad. They had dreams of building a house, however, and they saved and worked hard.

NHTSA (The National Highway Traffic Safety Administration) was the first to give Toney a contract after he went out on his own. They came through again.

The contract was to travel the East Coast of the United States speaking at high schools.

Toney and Donna were two newlyweds, jaunting around the U.S., having the time of their lives.

The contract with NHTSA went so well that Toney eventually received contracts from the states of Virginia, Maryland and Pennsylvania. Word was getting around about Toney's incredible message. Officials in these states wanted their citizens to benefit from his story.

Toney also did a lot of work with the military. He spoke at the Naval Academy in Annapolis, Maryland, and to the Marines at Camp LeJeune, North Carolina. Automobile accidents are the leading cause of death in the military. They appreciated Toney's message very much.

Suddenly, Toney and Donna's dreams of building a house were no longer dreams. He had good, steady work, and there was no sign of him slowing down.

They met with an architect to design their dream house. Toney wanted his new house to be completely accessible for himself, but he didn't want it filled with ramps and elevators. He asked the architect to design a home where someone on the outside would never know that a person in a wheelchair lived there.

Toney and Donna stayed on the road. He was reaching thousands of people each week. It was tiring, hard work, but it gave him an incredible feeling.

During Toney's extensive travels, he put many miles on his van. He eventually had to buy and customize a new one. All the hassle of setting up the new van so Toney could drive it was alleviated by his good friend, George Croft, owner of "Hoyt's Custom World" in Richmond. George spent hours with Toney setting the van up just the way he wanted it.

Toney spent a lot of time in Atlanta. He worked with a group there called "Arrive Alive Georgia." Their goals were to warn young people about the dangers of drinking and driving and to convince them to wear their safety belts. Toney fit nicely into their efforts.

While in Atlanta, Toney had the opportunity to visit Stone Mountain. This historical landmark became Toney's favorite place in the country.

The mountain includes a giant stone carving of Robert E. Lee, Stonewall Jackson, and Jefferson Davis. Toney admires their courage. A portrait of the mountain hangs in his den.

Toney and Donna's travels had their ups and downs. When you travel thousands of miles, things aren't always perfect. They always handled it, though.

During a tour through Alabama, Toney was stricken with a severe kidney infection. This is a common problem for the spinal cord injured.

But Toney does not have a typical wife. Donna stayed up night after night combatting his 103 degree temperature. She continuously bathed him in ice and fed him popsicles.

With the help of Donna's love and his determination, Toney never missed a program. What he had to say was too important.

Toney's contract in Pennsylvania went well. As a result, he received a contract from the Allegheny County Health Department.

Things were incredible. Toney's calendar was booked for months. People all over the country were hearing his message.

While in Allegheny, Toney gave a program where a safety manager from PPG Industries Inc was present. It turned out to be a very rewarding program.

The people at PPG Industries are remarkably safety conscious. They care deeply about their employees and, as it turned out, they care deeply about their community.

They contracted Toney for a month to speak within a hundred mile radius of Pittsburgh. He would give half the programs to PPG employees, and the other half were donated to school systems. PPG is a worldwide corporation. Toney was grateful to have that type of support.

Toney did not spend all of his time giving his program. He spent several days, in many states, speaking to state legislatures in support of the mandatory safety belt laws.

Toney told the legislatures his story and how a safety belt might have prevented his injuries. He also reminded them of another aspect of it all.

"A lot of people have a problem with the law because they feel like it infringes upon their rights. They feel it's their right to drive."

In reality it's not a right, it's a privilege. That privilege has to be governed. That's why we have drunk driving laws and speed limits. The safety belt law is just another step in the right direction to saving more lives."

That argument got to a lot of people, but his next point hit them even harder.

"Some people say 'If I'm in a crash who's it going to hurt but me?'

"Take my crash, for example. My hospital bills were over $125,000 the first year alone. I don't come from a wealthy family, and we had minimum insurance. Who do you think footed that bill? The taxpayers did. And this happens every day. So if you don't care about the human aspect of it all, look at it in dollars and cents."

Since then, the seat belt law has passed in several states. Toney feels proud to be a part of that.

Toney and Donna's months and months of travel were paying off. They spent night after night in hotels. Finally, they were able to spend a night in their very own home.

Their new house, built directly behind mama and daddy's, is absolutely breathtaking.

The long driveway seems to welcome you as you drive up. It's built on one level, but its high pitched roofs make it tremendous. Every room is gigantic, a wheelchair rider's delight. You don't need fingers to open the doors. The light switches are three foot high. And there's not a step in the house.

Toney and Donna picked up ideas for the design of the house while traveling the country. The slate foyer was an idea picked up in Georgia. The fireplace in their bedroom was from Pennsylvania. The house was one of a kind.

Toney and Donna each have their favorite rooms in the house. Donna loves her spacious kitchen, where she can practice her craft.

Toney loves his study. The room displays his personality. The walls are lined with plaques and awards he's received. One award that means a lot to Toney is a shiny silver cup that was presented to him by Virginia governor, Gerald Baliles. It's called the Commissioner's Cup, and Toney was the first recipient of this prestigious award for outstanding community service.

Two corners of the room display busts of Lincoln and Washington. He reads at a desk made for him, by hand, by our brother-in-law, Tate Jackson. Tate designed it so Toney could roll under it. He also designed the drawer handle so Toney could open it independently. It's his favorite piece of furniture.

A very satisfying thing about Toney and Donna's house was that they had done it all on their own. Many people had the misconception that he had received a large insurance settlement from his accident, which just wasn't true.

Over time, Toney's yard became very well-groomed. Toney couldn't do the work himself, but he had plenty of people who didn't mind helping him. Daddy loved working in the yard. Toney's friend Danny spent countless hours on the tractor.

Toney wanted to be a part of it all. He couldn't physically do the work, but he spent many hours in ninety degree heat supervising. As Danny would work on the tractor, Toney would read the instructions. As Danny planted trees, he would roll Toney all over the yard with him. That meant a lot to Toney.

As Toney and Donna stay on the road, mama and daddy watch

out for the house. Daddy gets their mail and waters Toney's trees. Mama winds Donna's clock and waters her plants.

As much as Toney and Donna loved their house, they didn't mind going on the road. Toney hoped his travels would never end.

The good folks at PPG knew the passion that Toney had for his program. They also knew that he was saving lives. They gave him another contract, this one for a nine month period. It would send him to many different states as well as into Canada. They again donated half the programs to the school systems.

Toney was ecstatic about this. It would give him the opportunity to see the country. But, most importantly, he would be able to spread his message to tens of thousands more people.

The trip to Canada was very rewarding for Toney. When they first began planning the trip, he was nervous about it. The thought of speaking in another country was overwhelming.It didn't take Toney long to realize that the same problems exist all across North America. In Canada, as in the U.S., there is a high highway death rate, a drunk driving problem, and even though each province has a safety belt law, many people still do not wear their safety belt on a regular basis.

The Canadians received Toney's program very well. People in different places may look, talk and dress differently, but when it comes down to it, people are people.

In Toney's program, he tries to make it clear that people shouldn't feel sorry for him.

"It's a good life for me, because I've adjusted to it, but I wouldn't recommend it to you."

After one program, a man came up to Toney with mixed emotions.

"I feel bad about your injury and for what you've been through, but I'm sure I'll leave here and put my safety belt on. I feel good. I've seen a person overcome a terrible tragedy and make something of his life. You give me hope."

Toney smiled.

That was exactly what he wanted to get across.

Toney and Donna's travels were paying big dividends. One trip to Pittsburgh reaped especially large benefits.

Toney spoke to half the students at a Pittsburgh high school one afternoon, with plans to speak again the following day.

That night, three young men who had been at the program went to a football game. As they left the driveway, they decided that what Toney had said made a lot of sense. They decided to buckle their safety belts.

On the way to the game, the driver of the car lost control and hit a house at a high speed.

A paramedic at the scene said had they not been wearing their safety belts, at least one of them probably would have been killed.

The next day, as Toney was preparing to speak to the other half of the students, the three young men came backstage. They had many cuts and abrasions. One of them had a bruise where the safety belt had caught him. They thanked Toney for saving their lives.

As he was leaving, Toney read the school sign on the front lawn.

"Our students thank Toney Lineberry."

Toney felt better than he ever had.

"This is what it's all about."

CHAPTER 11
STILL A CHAMPION

*T*he typical chatter of high school students bends my ear.
"Move Petey! I'm sitting there!"
"Forget it, rat face!"
"What's this assembly gonna be about?"
"I don't know. I heard it was something about a guy in a wheelchair."

As a piece of gum whizzed by my ear, I anxiously awaited the beginning of this program in Alabama. I hadn't seen Toney speak for a while. I looked forward to watching him silence this rowdy, Friday afternoon group of students.

Toney sat patiently backstage. He was very happy to be there. He took one last swig from his Mountain Dew as he was introduced. He took a deep breath and rolled on stage.

He looked incredibly sharp on this day. Not a hair was out of place. His clothes were perfectly pressed. The "L" on his tiepin sparkled from the light in the auditorium.

A few students continued to chatter as Toney began to speak.

"I want to talk to you today about a topic that's really important to all of us in our lives at this time. That topic is automobile safety."

The audience was filled with groans. "Oh no, not again."

Toney did not slow down to listen to the moaning students.

"First, I'd like to show you a few slides and tell you a story about my life. I'm not going to bore you with the whole thing, but I want to tell you about a portion of my life that's very important to me.

"Then, I'll share a few statistics with you. Not too many of those. I know they get kind of boring.

"Finally, I'd like to have a question and answer session. So the whole time I'm up here, be thinking of questions you'd like to ask me."

The lights went dim. The students became quiet as Donna cut on a slide projector showing a slide of Toney in a wrestling uniform. His big, muscular frame was quite a contrast to his now thin wheelchair-braced body.

Toney told of his wrestling days. The students seemed impressed that he was once a champion.

He told of his car. A slide flashed on the screen of the hot '69 Mustang. A slide of Toney and a pretty girl popped up next.

"I can't think of anyone is my high school class of two thousand who had it any better than me."

Toney then described that memorable, snowy day. Chills came over me as he refreshed my memory. He made it seem like yesterday.

The students seemed very interested as he continued by describing his ride to the party.

Toney's voice began to crack. "And then I noticed what looked like a river flowing across the road."

His words slowed. He sounded so sad. "But it was not a river." A slide of the mangled Mustang flashed on the screen. "It was a solid sheet of ice."

"Oh my God," I heard a student whisper.

Toney went on to describe the horror and pain he experienced down in that ravine. The students were on the edges of their seats. Toney made them feel as though they were in the car with him. They seemed especially shaken as he described what he thought were his friend's limbs wrapped around him.

"But when the rescue workers freed me from the wreckage, I noticed the arm flop down." Toney flopped his arm on his leg. "I noticed the leg flop to the ground. Suddenly I realized that it was my body they were moving, only I couldn't feel a thing."

Toney sounded so hurt, it was as if he was telling this story for the first time.

"I'll never walk again."

The lights went up. Some students rubbed their eyes as Toney continued. He had their emotions in the palm of his hand, and he wasn't going to let up.

"I know I paint a pretty ugly picture, at least I hope I do. Because I want each and every one of you to know that's exactly what this is, an ugly situation.

"When you see somebody in a wheelchair you probably think 'wow, that's got to be tough sitting in a wheelchair.' Some of you might not care, but if you are thinking that, you're right."

Toney's voice quickened.

"I'm not going to sit up here and try to kid you, it's tough not being able to walk. It's also tough not being able to feel anything from the chest down or move any of your ten fingers. The sad fact is it gets even uglier than that. Because it's also tough when you lose control of all bowel and bladder. It's gone. You have to learn how to deal with it and take care of it by artificial means."

Toney paused to adjust his body in his wheelchair. The students seemed to be thinking about his message.

"Thinking back on my accident, I have to think of ways it could have been prevented. I've thought about it and thought about it, and I've come up with three possible ways.

"First of all, it doesn't take a genius to figure out I should have never been on the road that night. I was warned over and over again. I took the car. It was 100 percent," Toney paused. He looked over the crowd and whispered "my fault."

"Second, anybody who had to be out that night—doctors, nurses, policemen—anybody who had to be somewhere, the maximum safe speed was twenty miles-per-hour. The estimated speed at the time of my crash was sixty-five miles-per-hour. So I was driving dangerously fast for the weather conditions."

A serious look traced Toney's face. He seemed almost desperate as he continued.

"Finally, and most importantly, and if you don't hear anything else I say today I beg you to please hear this. If I would have . . ." Toney paused. He seemed to be searching for just the right tone. "If I would have just had sense enough to buckle my safety belt, I

... I don't think I would be sitting up here today."

The students seemed to squirm in their seats as Toney stared at his knees. It was completely silent until he raised his head and continued.

"I've heard a lot of excuses for not wearing a safety belt. To be quite honest with you not too many of them make a whole lot of sense. There are just a couple I'd like to share with you to destroy some myths.

"When I first started studying automobile safety in general and the dynamics of a crash, I had to ask myself a question: 'Why did it take this to make me see that a safety belt probably could have helped me in that situation?' I've thought about it and thought about it, and I think I had the same excuse most people had: 'Hey, I'm a good driver. I'm in control. I'm not going to be in a crash. What are the chances of that happening to me?'

"Now that I've been there I kind of see it through a different pair of glasses. I know it can happen to me again, and it can happen to any one of you out there.

"The fact is one out of every five drivers will be in an automobile crash this year. Someone is killed in this country every ten minutes in an automobile crash. Someone is seriously injured or disabled every ten seconds. The chances of being in a crash are very great."

Toney's statistics did not bore the students. I could see one of them thinking about losing the one they care the most about.

"A lot of people have a fear of being trapped in a vehicle if their crashes involve fire or water. 'What if my car catches on fire or goes into a lake? I'll be trapped! I'll drown! I'll burn! I'm not wearing that crazy thing!' To those people, I have to say you've probably been watching too much television. Because in real life it's very rare that automobile crashes involve fire and water. In fact, less than one-half of one percent of all crashes involve fire or water. And there are thousands of crashes every day.

"The excuse that I hear most often for not wearing a safety belt, and the one I hate the most, is when people say 'You know Toney, the reason I don't wear that crazy thing is because it's just downright uncomfortable.

"Boy, I hate that one, but I hear it all the time. Well, to those people I have to say you may be right. It may be a little uncomfortable, until you get used to it. It may rub your waist or irritate your shoulder a little."

Again Toney's voice slowed. Tears seemed to form in his eye.

"But if you think that's uncomfortable, you ought to try being slammed into a steering column at sixty-five miles-per-hour.

"Or, better yet, you ought to try . . . try sitting in one of these for the rest of your life."

Toney stared at the wheels on his chair. He closed his eyes and sighed. I thought he was going to cry.

"This wheelchair is truly uncomfortable."

The students sat silent, just staring at Toney. I could see them pondering what he had said. "Maybe a safety belt isn't so uncomfortable after all," some of them must have been thinking.

"Briefly, I'd like to touch on another national problem that we're faced with. And I say national because it's out in California, it's down in Texas, and it's certainly in Virginia where I'm from. That problem is drunk driving.

"I'm getting to the point now when I speak to different groups and people ask 'What's the big deal about this drunk driving thing?'

"Let me briefly tell you what the big deal is. Approximately 46,000 people are killed every year on our nation's highways, 46,000 people. I don't know if you can fathom how many people that is. That's almost as many people who were killed in Vietnam. That's like a 727 jetliner going down every day for an entire year and everyone on board being killed.

"The sad fact is about half these deaths are alcohol related. Even sadder than that is that the majority of these involve young people."

Toney didn't want to preach to the students, but he wanted them to think about a few things.

"You're getting to a point in your lives when you've got to ask yourself a few questions. First, you've got to ask yourself 'Do I want to drink?' I can't decide for you, your teachers can't, your parents can't. If you choose to drink, that's your decision. I have no problem with that. I would like to tell you, if no one has already, that it's okay not to drink. It's okay.

"But if you should choose to drink, then you have to ask yourself another question. And that is: 'Do I want to drink and drive?' That one . . . That one I have a horrible problem with. Because when you mix alcohol and automobiles you come up with a dangerous weapon, and it's one that kills.

"So I beg you, please give it a whole lot of thought before you get behind the wheel intoxicated or get into a vehicle with someone who is. Because the results could truly be deadly."

Toney had touched on a very important subject in these students' lives. To many of them, drinking was very common. But Toney was not there to preach the evils of alcohol, he was there to prevent people from dying in automobiles.

"Now it's time for my favorite part of the program, and that's the question and answer session. Please feel free to ask me anything. I'll try my best to answer it. And if I can't, I'll try to find the answer somewhere."

Several students raised their hands. One asked Toney the question he usually received first.

"What happened to your friend who was in the crash with you?"

"I'm glad you asked me that," Toney answered. "Because I certainly wouldn't have left here without telling you about that. It's bad enough when you do something like this to yourself, but I think it's even harder to deal with injuring someone else or taking someone else's life."

The students sat silently, waiting to see if Toney's friend had been killed.

"In fact, I don't think I could deal with that. So I feel very fortunate that the boy who was riding with me actually ended up walking away from the crash."

A freckled girl in the front row asked the next question.

"What did your parents say when they found out you took the

car without their permission?"

"If I have any regrets at all about what has happened to me, it would have to be what I put my family through, especially my mom and dad."

As Toney continued, I thought about how special those two people he was referring to are.

"I can't even begin to fathom the horror my mom must have felt that night when the state trooper came to the house. He told her about my crash and that they didn't expect me to live.

"The following morning I saw my dad cry for the first time. My athletic ability meant more to him than it did to me.

"I will say this, they never said I told you so or called me stupid. They've always stood by me. They've done everything they could to rebuild my life."

Toney's tone changed to a sincere whisper. "And for that, I truly love them."

A teacher, standing in the back, asked the next question.

"What could your parents have done to keep you from going out against their wishes?"

"I'm often asked that question, so I've had plenty of time to think about it.

"I suppose they could have tied me up, maybe put me in the closet."

Some of the students laughed.

"But I probably would've still found a way out. I was eighteen, and in my mind I was an adult.

"In all due respect to my mom and dad, the automobile was never a dangerous thing to us. It was a tool to get from place to place. I never once saw my mom or dad wear a safety belt. I remember riding with them, looking over their shoulder, and seeing the speedometer at sixty-five.

"I guess what I'm saying is that parents need to set an example for their kids. They shouldn't tell their kids to wear their safety belts when they don't. They shouldn't tell their kids they'll take their driver's license away if they get a speeding ticket when they have a couple to their credit. Next question?"

"Were you drinking the night of your accident?"

"No, at that point I wasn't," Toney answered. "But I'm not going to lie to you, it was very common for me to ride around drinking with my friends.

"If I would've made it to the party, I'm sure I would have had two or three beers. Because in my mind I would have been saying 'A couple of beers is no big deal. I drive better after a few beers.' At that time I wasn't smart enough to know that one beer equals one ounce of liquor or one glass of wine. Alcohol is alcohol, and it all affects your driving greatly. I've learned that the hard way. Now I never drink and drive."

The principal asked the next question.

"How do you feel about air bags?"

"I'm for any new technology that can save someone's life or reduce injury. The air bag is very effective, but I don't think it's a replacement for the safety belt. For the bag to be completely effective, you still need to wear your safety belt. In my mind, your best protection would be to have both.

"I also feel that all automobiles should be equipped with shoulder harnesses in the back seat. The lap belt back there just isn't enough in high speed crashes.

"I want you all to know that safety belts aren't the only answer. You have to be a responsible driver. When you add up irresponsible acts—speeding, drinking and driving, following too close—your chances of survival are reduced a great deal."

The next question was another that Toney gets quite often.

"What ever happened to your girlfriend?"

"Well, that just didn't work out. I was young, she was young. When I got hurt, I was just no longer the person she had been dating."

I knew Toney wasn't through talking about this subject. I looked at his wonderful wife sitting beside me. She just smiled.

"But I'm a firm believer that things work out for the best. Because when that happened, I got over it. I went out and started meeting new people. And a few years ago I met this one real special girl."

Jokingly, Toney put his fist over his eye and pretended to blush. The students laughed as he continued.

"And I guess I . . . well, I fell in love."

The students let out one big "ahhh."

"So I asked her to marry me. And to my delight, she said yes. I'm very happy to introduce to you now my partner, my best friend, and most importantly, my wife, Donna."

Donna stood up as the students applauded. She looked so proud. She gave them a nod of thanks and smiled.

"I really wanted to introduce her," Toney said. "Because I couldn't be here without her. She does the paperwork. She does the scheduling. She dresses me. She puts me in this crazy chair every morning. She does all the work and I get to sit up here and have all the fun. We are 100 percent a team."

That led immediately into another question.

"Can you still have kids?"

"Some people with spinal cord injury can still have children. It all depends on your situation and degree of injury. Some can and some can't.

"It's one of those things that Donna and I would like to do someday. If we can't, we may very well adopt."

Another question came from the back.

"How did you start speaking to groups about your accident? What motivated you?"

"When I went through rehabilitation, I saw a lot of different types of tragedy. It made me want to try and prevent some of it.

"I started on a voluntary basis, but then I realized there was a need for it on a greater scale. I wanted to reach out more, so it became a full-time occupation. Along the way, I've learned from the very best in this field.

"Also, I've got a tremendous family. My mom and dad, my three older sisters, my younger brother and my wife, I know they'll never let me down. And I've got more friends than I can count. Without my family and friends I don't know where I'd be today. People don't see the support that's behind me."

Toney looked at his watch. He knew his time was about up.

"Finally, I didn't come here today to tell you what to do. I just wanted to share my experiences with you, and you can take it for what it's worth.

"All in all, I'm just trying to say two simple things. First, drinking and driving don't mix, drunk driving kills. Second, safety belts save lives.

"I wish each and every one of you a long, happy and healthy life."

The students jumped to their feet before Toney could finish. The auditorium seemed to shake as they clapped and cheered for him.

I stayed in my seat, my body absorbed in chills. I thought back to Toney stomping off a wrestling mat, his fist thrust in the air. I remembered the crowd standing and screaming for their champion.

I looked at my smiling brother up on that stage. I realized that he was, once again, a champion.

Toney Speaks Across North America

If you would like Toney to address your school, business, or civic group, or order additional copies of this book, please contact him at the following address:

> Toney Lineberry
> Professional Consultant On Highway Safety
> 570 Seay Road
> Manakin-Sabot, Virginia 23103

About The Author

Tom Lineberry is now a senior at Old Dominion University in Norfolk, Virginia. He will receive a degree in political science and a certificate in paralegal studies in May, 1988.

He plans to pursue a career in law and will be attending the T. C. Williams School of Law at the University of Richmond.

He hopes to further his writing career and is currently working on a novel.